TERRORISM

edited by STEVEN ANZOVIN

THE REFERENCE SHELF

Volume 58 Number 3

THE H. W. WILSON COMPANY

New York   1986

THE REFERENCE SHELF

The books in this series contain reprints of articles, excerpts from books, and addresses on current issues and social trends in the United States and other countries. There are six separately bound numbers in each volume, all of which are generally published in the same calendar year. One number is a collection of recent speeches; each of the others is devoted to a single subject and gives background information and discussion from various points of view, concluding with a comprehensive bibliography. Books in the series may be purchased individually or on subscription.

Library of Congress Cataloging in Publication Data

Main entry under title:

Terrorism.

    (The Reference shelf ; v. 58, no. 3)
    Bibliography: p.
    1. Terrorism.   2. Terrorism in mass media.
3. Terrorists.   4. Terrorism—Prevention.   I. Anzovin,
Steven.   II. Series.
HV6431.T444   1986   303.6'25   86–11126
ISBN 0-8242-0725-4

Printed in the United States of America

CONTENTS

PREFACE

The use of terror to attain political goals is not new. All oppressive governments have found terror to be an effective means of social control. In ancient Judea, for example, the Romans crucified civilians by the hundreds as a way of instilling fear and obedience in the populace. State terrorism has hardly changed in philosophy or methods since the time of the Romans, although most states that practice internal terrorism refer to it by a euphemism such as "maintenance of national security."

This book is primarily concerned with another kind of terrorism—violence by individuals and organizations for political purposes. Today, as Walter Laqueur notes, terrorism is "an insurrectional strategy that can be used by people of very different political convictions. . . . As the technology of terrorism can be mastered by people of all creeds, so does its philosophy transcend the traditional dividing lines between political doctrines. It is truly all-purpose and value-free." There has been a sharp rise in the number of plane hijackings, assassinations, and machine-gun and hand-grenade attacks, in large part because of developments that have also increased international trade: better communications, rapid transportation, the availability of improved products—in this case, compact and deadly weapons—and the commitment of resources by sympathetic governments.

Some terrorists have an authentic and fanatical commitment to a cause; others claim to be acting in the service of a cause, but in fact are nihilists for whom bloodshed is an end in itself. In recent years there has also been a proliferation of groups that combine fanaticism in ideology with cold, rational professionalism in the planning and execution of violent acts. All kinds of terrorists share an inability to see people as individuals, rather than as representatives of a political or religious system; hence their willingness to kidnap, torture, and murder complete strangers in order to intimidate distant governments. For terrorists, no one—not even a child—is innocent.

5

The United States, whose citizens have been the targets of nearly half of all terrorist acts in the past few years, faces an especially difficult dilemma. A recent *New York Times* poll showed that during and immediately after recent terrorist incidents the majority of Americans wanted their leaders to strike back hard at the terrorists. The same respondents, however, were reluctant to endanger the lives of hostages by high-risk rescue attempts or retaliatory strikes. In addition, many Americans are unwilling to have their freedom to travel, and their domestic civil liberties, curtailed. These contradictory demands are the source of much of the terrorists' power over us; not only do we not know where and when they will strike, or what they want, but we also do not know how to stop them without sacrificing things we value.

The articles, essays, speeches, and discussions reprinted in this volume present several important aspects of this baffling problem. Section I is a general introduction to the nature of terrorism today: its definition, recent history, and its devastating effect on the social fabric of one nation, Lebanon. An important and frustrating aspect of contemporary terrorism is its ability to draw on the resources of established states that harbor terrorists and support their activities as part of an aggressive foreign policy. As the speeches and articles in Section II reveal, this poses intractable problems for nations seeking to put a stop to terrorism. Section III discusses ways that terrorism should *not* be fought. The inadequacy of most antiterrorist policies, and the poor coordination between nations involved in terrorist incidents, are made worse by the news media, which often give terrorists a free public forum to state their "case." The final section is devoted to more effective ways to deal with terrorism, domestic and foreign. Most commentators believe, however, that terrorism is likely to be an abiding problem in our world.

The editor would like to thank the authors and publishers who have kindly granted permission to reprint the material in this collection. Special thanks are also due to the Englewood (New Jersey) Public Library and to Diane Podell of the B. Davis Schwartz Memorial Library, C. W. Post Center, Long Island University.

STEVEN ANZOVIN

April 1986

I. TERROR IN THE MODERN WORLD

EDITOR'S INTRODUCTION

Every few months, the world (or that portion of the world where a free press operates) is given another opportunity to ponder the problem of terrorism. Crisis follows crisis; when the aftershocks of one incident have begun to die away, it is only a matter of time until another one explodes into the news. Terrorism is becoming commonplace.

The definition of terrorism is still a matter of debate. Fundamentally, terrorism consists of the use of violence, in a nonmilitary context, to achieve political goals. Its primary objective usually is not to capture territory or personnel, as in a war, but rather to communicate a threat to someone other than the victim. Intimidation through violence is a common tool of those who seek power or an extension of power, as useful on a school playground as in a revolution.

The current state of thinking about modern forms of terrorism—what we know and what we do not know—is the subject of Brian M. Jenkins's "Statements about Terrorism," reprinted from the *Annals of the American Academy of Political and Social Science*. Although the environmental factors that facilitate terrorism are reasonably well understood, Jenkins points out that "the rhetoric against terrorism almost always exceeds the amount of resources devoted to combating it." Some of the unpublicized successes of the various Western governments in foiling terrorist attacks are mentioned in Robert B. Oakley's address "Terrorism: Overview and Developments," which looks at the rise of new groups and new tactics over the past fifteen years. The third selection, "The Power of the Fanatics," a *New York Times* article by Thomas L. Friedman, describes how it feels to be a victim of terrorist violence. As a journalist stationed in Beirut, Friedman had many opportunities to observe terrorism in action—both government-sponsored terrorism, such as the massacre of Syrian villagers

by the Syrian army, and violence committed by gunmen belonging
to political organizations. Indeed, while most people in the United
States, and in the West in general, know terrorism only through
news reports, Lebanon is an example of a society where terrorism
has become the norm.

STATEMENTS ABOUT TERRORISM[1]

Any prediction ten years ago that terrorists would seize 50 embassies and consulates, take over the headquarters of the Organization of Petroleum Exporting Countries (OPEC) in Vienna and
hold the oil ministers of 11 nations hostage, kidnap hundreds of
diplomats and businessmen and collect hundreds of millions of
dollars in ransom, kidnap and murder the former premier of Italy,
assassinate Lord Mountbatten and President Sadat, and try to assassinate the President of France, the commander of the North Atlantic Treaty Organization (NATO), and even the Pope, would
have been regarded as the stuff of novels, not headlines.

Terrorism has proved to be a far more serious problem than
we anticipated 10 or 12 years ago.

Terrorism has commanded the attention of governments and
attracted the attention of scholars. After more than 10 years of terrorism to observe and nearly 10 years of research on the topic,
what can we say about it? I would like to review what we know
about terrorism, and what trends are discernible. Before doing
that, however, we must deal with the problem of definition.

The term "terrorism" has no precise or widely accepted definition. The problem of definition is compounded by the fact that
"terrorism" has become a fad word, used promiscuously and often
applied to a variety of acts of violence that are not strictly terrorism. The term is generally pejorative. Some governments label as
terrorism all violent acts committed by their political opponents,

[1]Reprint of an article by Brian M. Jenkins, director of the Security and Subnational Conflict Program
of The Rand Corporation. *Annals of the American Academy of Political and Social Science.* 463:11+. S. '82.
All rights reserved. Reprinted by permission.

while anti-government extremists frequently claim to be the victims of government terror. Thus, what terrorism is seems to depend on one's point of view. Use of the term implies a moral judgment; if a party can successfully attach the label of terrorist to its opponent, then it has indirectly persuaded others to adopt its moral viewpoint.

The difficulty of defining terrorism has led to the cliché that one man's terrorist is another man's freedom fighter, implying that there can be no objective definition of terrorism, no universal standards of conduct in peace or war. I reject that.

Most civilized nations have identified modes of conflict that are criminal—homicide, kidnapping, threats to life, the willful destruction of property, and so on. Laws against such criminal acts may be violated in war, but even in war there are rules that outlaw the use of certain weapons and tactics.

The rules of war grant civilian noncombatants at least theoretical immunity from deliberate attack; they prohibit taking civilian hostages and they prohibit actions against those held captive; they recognize neutral territory. But terrorists recognize no neutral territory, no noncombatants, no bystanders. They seize, threaten, and often murder hostages. One man's terrorist is everyone's terrorist.

Terrorism is best defined by the quality of the acts, not by the identity of the perpetrators or the nature of their cause. All terrorist acts are crimes. Many would also be violations of the rules of war, if a state of war existed. All involve violence or the threat of violence, usually directed against civilian targets. The motives of most terrorists are political, and terrorist actions are generally carried out in a way that will achieve maximum publicity. The perpetrators are usually members of an organized group, and unlike other criminals, they often claim credit for their acts. Finally, a terrorist act is intended to produce effects beyond the immediate physical damage it causes.

This definition of terrorism does not limit the application of the term to actions by nongovernmental groups. Governments may also be terrorist, and it makes little difference to the victim whether he is kidnapped and murdered by a gang of anti-government extremists or by gunmen employed by the secret police. Government terror tends to be primarily internal, however, and most incidents of international terrorism are carried out by nongovernmental groups, although they may have direct or indirect state support.

International terrorism comprises those incidents that have clear international consequences: incidents in which terrorists go abroad to strike their targets, select victims or targets because of their connections to a foreign state (diplomats, executives of foreign corporations), attack airliners on international flights, or force airliners to fly to another country.

I do not for a moment think that these comments have disposed of the issue of definition. Doubtless, it will come up again. Let us put it aside for the moment, however, and proceed with a review of trends in terrorism.

The Level of Terrorist Violence

The use of terrorist violence has increased significantly during the last 14 years. The number of recorded incidents oscillates from year to year, but the overall trajectory is clearly upward, and the increase is not merely a reflection of better reporting; it is genuine.

Terrorism has also increased in severity. The number of fatalities and other casualties resulting from terrorist attacks has climbed. Of greater significance is the fact that the number of terrorist incidents resulting in multiple fatalities has increased both in actual number and as a percentage of the total number of incidents.

Despite these increases, terrorists continue to operate within limits. Most terrorist incidents involve no casualties. They are purely symbolic acts of violence. The median of those incidents with fatalities is close to one. With the exception of a few incidents such as the 1980 bombing of the Bologna train station in which 84 people were killed, terrorists have not entered the domain of mass murder or carried out schemes that could cause widespread disruption.

Within its present limits, terrorism is bearable. This is not to say that terrorism is tolerable, for it has become a more serious problem than anticipated. Yet few governments are seriously imperiled. Society survives. Terrorism is a pain, not a mortal danger.

The Spread of Terrorist Violence

The use of terrorist tactics is spreading throughout the world. The number of countries in which terrorist incidents have taken place has increased.

Terrorism affects the world unequally. Although the problem is widespread—the Rand Corporation's chronology of international terrorism records incidents in 117 countries since 1968—a handful of countries suffer a disproportionate share of terrorist activities. Approximately half of the recorded incidents have occurred in only 10 countries.

Most of the incidents take place in Western Europe, followed by Latin America, the Middle East and North Africa, then North America. Few incidents occur in Eastern Europe, Asia, or the Pacific region.

The Environment of Terrorism

There are many hypotheses that attribute the cause of terrorism to social, economic, cultural, technological, and geographical factors, but no single factor can be identified as a universal cause of terrorism or even as a universal precipitating factor.

Some environments, however, clearly are not propitious. Totalitarian states provide a poor environment for terrorism.

There are many factors that contribute to an environment propitious for terrorism: the mobility provided by modern jet travel; access to a global audience through the news media; the vulnerabilities of modern society; the availability of weapons and explosives; perceived injustice; deep-rooted ethnic, ideological, and religious divisions; the failure of other modes of dissent or influence; historical traditions of political violence; ideologies that condone violence; unresponsive or insensitive governments; sharply circumscribed or ineffective security forces; the high value that most societies place on human life, which constrains governments from totally ignoring the fate of hostages held by terrorists; the historically unprecedented respect shown in the world today for the concept of national sovereignty, even for the sovereignty of those nations that provide sanctuary and aid to terrorists; the growing number of nations that no longer abide by the rules of international conduct and that support terrorists or dispatch assassination squads; the "legitimization" of terrorism itself as a mode of conduct.

In no country are all of these ingredients present. Terrorism results from idiosyncratic combinations of factors.

The Tactics of Terrorism

Terrorists operate with a very limited tactical repertoire. Bombings alone account for roughly half of all terrorist incidents. Six basic tactics comprise 95 percent of the total: bombings, assassinations, armed assaults, kidnappings, barricade and hostage situations, and hijackings. No terrorist group uses all of them.

Approximately one-third of all terrorist incidents involve hostages. Terrorists seize hostages to gain attention and to increase their leverage by placing human lives in the balance.

The terrorists' tactical repertoire has changed little over time. Hijacking airliners and seizing embassies to make political demands are two significant terrorist inventions, along with kidnapping and leg-shooting. Some terrorist groups have experimented with other forms of attack—for example, poisoning oranges—but most groups stick to familiar tactics.

Terrorists appear more imitative than innovative. New tactics, once they are introduced, are likely to be widely imitated.

The Targets of Terrorism

Terrorist attacks are directed almost entirely against civilian targets, individuals who in any other mode of conflict would be regarded as noncombatants. Only about 6 percent of the incidents listed in the Rand chronology were directed against military or police officials, for example, military attachés. Certainly, blowing up a social worker in a car with his children on the way to school because he is a part-time reserve police officer is an act that belongs within the domain of terrorism rather than combat.

Diplomats are the most common target in incidents of international terrorism, and increasingly so. Terrorist attacks against diplomatic personnel and facilities increased by 60 percent in 1980 and 1981 over the previous two-year period.

Businessmen are also frequent targets of terrorists. Terrorists attack businessmen as symbols of economic systems they oppose or of foreign domination. They kidnap executives or threaten corporations to finance further terrorist operations. In the past 10 years, terrorists have collected between $125 million and $250 million in ransom payments.

The Terrorists

Terrorists share a common demographic profile. The typical terrorist is male—although there are numerous notable exceptions—in his early twenties, single, from a middle- or upper-class urban family, well educated, with some university training.

We know far less about the terrorist's mindset. Do terrorists think differently from the way you or I think? Is there a type of personality predisposed to terrorism? Little systematic research has been done in this area. Indeed, what we know about the terrorist mind today is roughly equivalent to what we knew about Africa in the middle of the nineteenth century. We knew the general shape of the continent, and a few explorers had traveled up African rivers and returned with their observations. But for the most part, it remained *terra incognita* for Europeans, a dark continent. So it is with the terrorist mindset today. We have a few notions, some assumptions, and some assertions, but some of the ideas seem as fanciful as those demons and sea monsters that ancient cartographers put at the far edge of what they knew. The growing population of terrorists who have written memoirs, given interviews while still on the run, or talked in prison has provided glimpses into the interior, and a few scholarly inquiries have been made. What can we say about them?

For one thing, there appears to be no identifiable psychotic personality. Most terrorists are not crazy in the clinical sense. Indeed, there may be nothing psychiatrically unexpected about terrorists.

Most terrorists appear to share certain common attitudes. Observers generally agree that terrorists are for the most part true-believers, absolutists who see the world in black and white, us versus them. They are uncompromising, action-prone, willing—sometimes even eager—to take risks. Whether these traits are present in an individual before he joins a terrorist group or whether they develop as a result of being in a terrorist group is not clear.

Terrorists do not become terrorists overnight. It is a long process that begins with alienation, perhaps mixed with boredom, proceeds to protest and permanent dissidence, and ends with going underground as a member of a terrorist group.

Observers agree that terrorists have many problems, something we tend to overlook. They suffer depression. They may feel as uncomfortable with their role in a terrorist group as they did with their role in society. They have neurotic fears of succeeding. They strive to inflate their own importance by adopting grandiose postures or engaging in histrionic behavior. They lose sight of reality and come to believe their own propaganda, overestimating their own strength, their appeal, the weakness of their enemies, the imminence of victory. At the same time, they are not immune to disillusionment with their group or its cause. Some quit. Others want to. But getting out of a terrorist group is hard to do, much harder than joining one. It requires an admission by the terrorist that he has been wrong. It involves physical risk, in that his former comrades may brand him a traitor and try to kill him. He may have to remain on the run from both police and the terrorists.

Terrorists have failed to articulate a comprehensive strategy for taking power. They are bombers and shooters, tacticians at best, not strategists.

Terrorist groups have increased their links, providing each other with expressions of support, training, weapons, and asylum, occasionally participating in joint operations or proxy operations. Still there is no evidence of a single brain. Relationships are loose. Terrorists boast of more cohesion than actually exists in an attempt to appear more powerful than they are.

Terrorist groups change over time. Ideology declines as violent action becomes an end in itself. Members who survive, brutalized by the long struggle and the loss of comrades, tend to become more ruthless in their tactics. New members, some of whom are common criminals recruited in the prisons and thugs attracted to terrorist activity for entirely personal rather than political motives, change the composition of a group and the mindset of its members.

Many terrorist groups engage in ordinary criminal activity to support themselves. In time, terrorist groups increasingly come to resemble ordinary criminal organizations operating under a thin political veneer. Kidnappers keep the ransom they collect for themselves, and "Godfathers" skim cash from protection rackets.

The Government Response to Terrorism

Terrorists have occasionally won concessions and some have provoked the overthrow of governments, but terrorist tactics alone have failed to bring terrorists to power. Terrorism remains an ingredient, not a recipe, for seizing power. Over the long run, governments have prevailed over the terrorists.

We cannot really say that democracy has been imperiled by terrorism. Authoritarian regimes have characteristically reacted to terrorist threats with repressive measures, while nations with strong democratic institutions and traditions have cautiously limited certain liberties as the price of security—making travelers undergo screening procedures at airports, for example.

Terrorism diverts government attention for brief moments of crisis. When not under the gun, most governments treat terrorism as no more than a nuisance. This makes planning and preparation difficult.

In the United States and most Western European countries, combating terrorism has low priority. The rhetoric against terrorism almost always exceeds the amount of resources devoted to combating it.

Although governments have a clear advantage over the long run, they are almost always at a disadvantage in dealing with individual episodes. Terrorists create dramas in which they and their victims are the central figures. Except for an occasional successful commando rescue, governments seldom get to play the role of the hero. More often, governments are seen as reactive, impotent, incompetent. Intelligence has failed, security has been breached. The government is unable to satisfy the public's appetite for action against the terrorists.

Public perceptions of government standing and competence in combating terrorism are based not on the government's overall performance but rather on its performance in a few dramatic hostage incidents in which it suffers disadvantages from the moment the incident occurs. The public sees the government only in crisis, demonstrably unable to provide security for its citizens, sometimes yielding to the terrorists to save lives, often unable to bring its enemies to justice. Such perceptions may corrode the links between the governed and the governments and may contribute to public support for drastic measures to counter terrorism.

Governments have developed specialized capabilities for dealing with terrorism. Security has been increased. Specialized tactics and skills have been developed for use in hostage situations. Negotiators have been trained. The behavioral sciences have made a major contribution to this aspect of the terrorist problem. Crisis management procedures have been developed, and specially trained military units have been created.

The development of negotiating skills does not imply a greater willingness to bargain with terrorists holding hostages. More and more governments have adopted hard-line, no concessions, no negotiations policies in dealing with terrorists.

Governments have also demonstrated an increased willingness to use force in resolving terrorist incidents at home and abroad. Specially trained units have successfully used force in rescuing hostages held aboard hijacked airliners and in embassies. The willingness to use force may have some deterrent effect, but the evidence in that direction is barely perceptible. There has, however, been a recent decline in embassy takeovers.

We may have arrived at or come pretty close to the limits of international cooperation in combating terrorism. In spite of the problems that remain, it appears that unless terrorism takes new directions, progress in international cooperation will continue to be limited, with emphasis on the details of implementation.

State Support of Terrorism

A number of states provide financial support, arms, training, asylum, and other forms of assistance to various terrorist groups.

State support appears to be more important to terrorist groups operating on foreign territory. Indigenous terrorist groups obtain most of their support from domestic sources. A growing number of governments themselves are using terrorist tactics, employing terrorist groups, or exploiting terrorist incidents to wage war on foreign foes or domestic enemies living abroad.

The Effects of Terrorism on Society

Few efforts have been made to measure systematically the effects of terrorism on society. Except for a few public opinion polls, we have only individual observations to rely on. What do these tell us?

Unlike their governments, most people consider terrorism to be a very serious problem. This is true even in countries that have not experienced high levels of terrorism.

Terrorism provokes backlash and polarization, and hardens attitudes. A series of polls conducted in Western European countries between February 1970 and November 1977, a period of growing terrorism, show a steady erosion of support for the statement that "our society must be gradually improved by reform" and growing support for the statement that "our present society must be valiantly defended against all subversive force."

A majority of people appear to support harsher action against terrorists than governments have been willing to impose. Public opinion polls indicate widespread support for military reprisals, the assassination of terrorist leaders, capital punishment, and summary executions, even if these measures limit civil liberties or endanger innocent civilians.

The impression that governments cannot provide basic security has become more widespread.

Terrorism has seriously eroded the quality of life in many places, including Northern Ireland, Lebanon, Israel, Turkey, Uruguay, Argentina, and El Salvador.

Terrorism has affected the life-styles and work habits of political leaders, diplomats, and corporate executives.

The Future of Terrorism

Although under pressure from increasingly skillful authorities, the indigenous terrorist groups that appeared in Europe in the late 1960s and early 1970s have survived: the Irish Republican Army (IRA), the Basque ETA, the Red Army Faction, and the Red Brigade. That such groups could survive for more than a decade in an unfriendly urban environment in a modern nation is a surprise.

The survival of many of the older terrorist groups who have been on the scene for a decade or more, plus the appearance of new groups emulating the model provided by the first generation of terrorist groups, suggests that terrorism is likely to be a long-range, perhaps a chronic problem.

Will terrorists escalate? There are certain pressures in that direction—the increasing resistance of governments, the declining news value of terrorist incidents as they become commonplace— but there is no inexorable progression from what terrorists have done so far to acts of greater magnitude. Technical limitations or self-imposed constraints have kept terrorists out of the realm of mass destruction. Although some minor escalation can be seen in the increased number of terrorist incidents resulting in multiple fatalities, we simply cannot say whether or not terrorists will exploit new weapons or new targets to create greater destruction or disruption.

TERRORISM: OVERVIEW AND DEVELOPMENTS[2]

It was 15 years ago today that a major new chapter in international terrorist spectaculars literally exploded on the world scene. Palestinian terrorists from the radical PFLP [Popular Front for the Liberation of Palestine] faction hijacked four airliners and

[2]Address by Ambassador Robert Oakley, director of the Department of State's Office for Counterterrorism and Emergency Planning, before the Issues Management Association, Chicago, September 13, 1985. *Department of State Bulletin.* 85:61–5. N. '85.

forced the pilots to fly three of them to a former World War II RAF [Royal Air Force] base in Jordan—Dawson Field. On September 13, 1970, they blew the planes up before the cameras. A fourth plane already had been blown up in Cairo. Those blazing explosions marked a new dimension in the ability of terrorists to catch our attention and make terrorism an act of macabre theater as well as deadly crime.

That mass hijacking attack brought the terrorist groups to the front pages—and, more important to them—to the prime-time evening television news around the world.

That spectacular did not benefit the terrorists in the short term. It led to King Hussein's expulsion of the PLO [Palestine Liberation Organization] from Jordan amid heavy fighting which cost hundreds, if not thousands, of Palestinian lives. However, the events of September 1970, which prompted one terrorist group to take on the name "Black September," set into motion a chain of events in Lebanon and elsewhere which are still unfolding. These range from the 1972 Olympic tragedy in Munich, the attack upon Lod Airport in Israel, all the way to current terrorist actions by Palestinians in the Middle East and Europe. Some of them are Palestinian vs. Palestinian, with mainline PLO and Jordanian officials targeted by dissident Palestinian groups, some of which receive help from Syria.

During the 1970s, West European terrorists struck at their own targets—the IRA [Irish Republican Army] assassinated Lord Mountbatten and killed hundreds of innocent people in Northern Ireland and Britain. Italian terrorists, notably the Red Brigades, killed former Prime Minister Moro, and scores of Italians became innocent victims. West German terrorists—the Red Army Faction—robbed banks, planted their bombs, killed, and kidnaped.

Today, new groups which were virtually unknown on the international terrorist scene a few years ago have suddenly emerged alongside the older groups to take their toll of lives.

• Muslim fundamentalist Shi'a terrorists, inspired by the Ayatollah Khomeini's "Islamic revolution" and supported by the Iranian Government, have committed suicide bombings against the U.S. Marine barracks and Embassy buildings in Lebanon and carried out attacks in Kuwait, including the U.S. Embassy, the French Embassy, and Kuwaiti facilities.

• Sikh terrorists have assassinated Prime Minister Indira Ghandi and several other Indian officials, apparently planted the bombs which blew up the Air India 747 in mid-air and exploded at Tokyo's Narita Airport, and tried to conduct assassinations in the United States.

• In Latin America, leftist guerrilla groups and narcotics traffickers have used terrorists to attack and threaten U.S. ambassadors and other officials as well as local government leaders in several Latin American countries.

Some forms of terrorism had appeared to be on the decline, such as aircraft hijacking. But Shi'a terrorists last year revived that technique, which had been used by the Palestinians. Two American Government employees were killed when the terrorists hijacked a Kuwaiti airliner to Iran last December. A Jordanian airliner was hijacked and—in echoes of Dawson Field—blown up at Beirut airport this summer. And, of course, there was the hijacking of TWA 847 in June—the first time an American plane had been hijacked in the Middle East since a Pan Am plane was blown up during that September 1970 attack. Kidnapings had also appeared to be on the decline, but in the past 2 years seven Americans have been kidnaped in Beirut and remain as captives. A U.S. businessman was kidnaped in Bogota, Colombia, last month. And President Duarte's daughter has just been taken this week in El Salvador.

Nevertheless, the principal terrorist tactics in the past 2 years have been bombings and armed attacks with an increasing intent to kill, maim, and injure—not merely to frighten or inflict property damage. We have seen this in West Germany where a Red Army Faction car bomb, 5 weeks ago, killed and injured Americans and Germans alike at a U.S. Air Force base near Frankfurt, and an American serviceman was brutally murdered for his identification card. In Madrid this week, an American businessman died of injuries received while jogging nearby as Basque terrorists set off a bomb which wounded some 16 Spanish policemen.

I mention these points not with the intention of providing a comprehensive overview—it would take more time than you have and a better memory or files than I have. Nor do I want to scare you into abandoning travel or business operations abroad for a retreat into fortress America. Rather, this brief introduction is meant to help illustrate one of the major problems in countering international terrorism—its shifting patterns and cycles—as well as to accentuate the need for security preparedness. Terrorism is a form of warfare in which unpredictability and surprise are major weapons. Those who indulge in this form of ripping at the thin veneer of civilization hide behind sneak attacks and faceless phone calls. Their favorite targets are usually not military or police installations but unarmed and unsuspecting civilians, particularly diplomats—and businessmen.

Terrorism is not a new scourge. It is too easy to forget that even terrorism has a history and that some of the terrorists of today are following trends set hundreds of years ago and set in the same part of the world. In the Middle East, terrorism has been known at least since the 1st century A.D. during the Zealots' struggle against the Romans in ancient Palestine. In the 11th century A.D., the Assassins sect emerged in Persia and spread to Syria where they attacked the Christian crusaders as well as other local officials.

The Barbary pirates conducted their own form of terrorism, operating from what is now Libya and leading to the landing by the U.S. Marines on the shores of Tripoli a century and a half ago. The forerunner of the car bomb, the cart bomb, was reported in Napoleonic times.

The more modern versions of terrorism and its ideological underpinnings emerged in the latter part of the 19th century, particularly in Russia and other European countries. The German radical, Karl Heinzen, of the mid-19th century wrote: "If you have to blow up half a continent and pour out a sea of blood in order to destroy the Barbarians, have no scruples of conscience." The leftist terrorist groups in Europe, such as the German Red Army Faction, appear to have inherited this sort of pseudo-intellectual rationalization for their violent attacks upon society.

Current Trends

Terrorism has ebbed and flowed, but today the number of incidents is greater than before, and it is increasingly a worldwide phenomenon. In 1984, there were more than 600 international terrorist incidents, a 20% increase over the average level of the previous 5 years. The number of incidents is up further this year—480 for the first 8 months, compared with 382 for the same period last year.

Here are some of the trends we are likely to see over the next few years:

✓ **First**, international terrorism is and will remain a prominent factor on the international political landscape, despite the intensified efforts we and other governments are making. Terrorism will not easily disappear for many reasons: a worldwide system of competitive arms sales makes modern weapons available more easily to terrorist groups; mass communications assure instantaneous publicity for terrorist acts; travel is easier between different countries, and border controls are diminishing, particularly in Western Europe; the copycat phenomenon causes more and more desperate or amoral individuals and groups to adopt terrorism; and, most important, in an age when weapons of mass destruction as well as increasingly lethal conventional armaments have made regular warfare too costly, terrorism is viewed by certain countries as a cheap way to strike a blow at their enemies with little or no retaliatory action.

✓ **Second**, for the United States the problem is likely to continue to be much more external than internal. Incidents within the United States, especially externally connected terrorism, have been decreasing, altogether representing less than 1% of the world total, whereas the United States abroad has been the number one target for terrorists. This is due, in large part, to the exceedingly effective work of the FBI [Federal Bureau of Investigation], generally tighter controls on visas and at U.S. points of entry, and an aversion by the American people to foreign-inspired violence.

Domestic terrorism is a serious problem, with the principal threats coming from Puerto Rican terrorists plus individuals and groups, often loosely linked, who reflect inchoate neo-Nazi, white supremacy attitudes. But the effective work of the FBI and local law enforcement agencies has kept it from getting out of hand.

There is a potential foreign terrorist threat of major dimensions within the United States, particularly from several Moslem and other ethnic groups (e.g. Libyan, Iranian, Palestinian, Armenian, etc.). Excellent work by the FBI, other law en[...]ment agencies, and our intelligence community, plus fear by the state sponsors of terrorism of the consequences were they to be caught supporting attacks within the United States, have kept this threat under control so far. However, we can never feel safe, never slacken vigilance, as shown by the FBI prevention this spring of planned attacks in this country by Sikh and Libyan terrorists and its arrest last month of Puerto Rican terrorists linked to Cuba.

Third, open societies will remain the principal targets of terrorists, although no societies are immune. Democratic societies are vulnerable to terrorism, on the one hand, because the terrorists might succeed more easily in bringing the democratic governments to their knees due to their very openness and concern for their citizens; or, on the other hand, overreaction by a democratic state to the threat could destroy the very nature of the society. Terrorists would welcome either outcome.

The means of attack which are increasingly available to the opponents of democratic states are also available, to a lesser degree, to the opponents of dictatorships. They may have tighter controls at home where basic freedoms do not count, but they are vulnerable abroad, and during 1984 the Soviet Union ranked number seven on the international terrorist victim list. This is far behind the United States and other free countries, probably because most groups abroad are vaguely leftist or Marxist in ideology. We have little evidence of direct Soviet support to such terrorist groups. However, their objectives clearly parallel those of the U.S.S.R., and they receive indirect support and encouragement.

Fourth, there has been an unmistakable rise in state-supported terrorism over the past few years, with Iran, Libya, Syria, Cuba, and Nicaragua as the most active, determined, systematic supporters of terrorist groups and activities. The combination of direct government assistance in arms, explosives, communications, travel documents, and training with fanatic individuals or groups goes a long way to explaining the shift in tactics toward bombing and armed attack and the accompanying increase in the casualty rates from terrorist attack. The fact that the states

I have mentioned—except Iran—receive large quantities of Soviet arms, which, in turn, flow directly to the terrorists, is hardly coincidental.

Fifth, there is a trend toward greater lethality. To date, terrorists have, by and large, used conventional methods of attack (high explosives, firearms, hand grenades, car bombs, etc.) with great effect. However, as our defenses against conventional weapons improve, so does the likelihood that terrorist groups will move to more sophisticated and esoteric methods of attack. The potential impact to our society and to our national security is catastrophic in nature. (In recognition of the enormity of the potential, we have been developing interagency plans for the response to and the countering of plausible terrorist threat in either nuclear or chemical/biological attack.)

The Current International Terrorist Scene

Looking behind these trends in more detail at the international terrorist scene, we note that the Middle East has become the primary source of international terrorism, accounting for about 35% of the incidents. But international travel has permitted the export of Middle Eastern terrorism elsewhere. There are two main categories of Middle Eastern terrorists:

First, fanatical Palestinians who have split off from the mainline PLO led by Arafat and often have the direct support of Libya and Syria; and

Second, Shi'a zealots residing in many Arab countries, especially Lebanon, who are inspired, trained, and often armed, financed, and, to varying degrees, guided by Iran. They have bombed the U.S. Embassy and Marines and the French military in Beirut, hijacked U.S. and French aircraft, and taken U.S., French, British, and other nationals hostage. They are responsible for terrorist activities against various Arab states.

In addition, Libya is becoming an increasing threat to its neighbors in North Africa, to many states in black Africa, and to peace and stability in the Middle East, using propaganda and subversion or overt military attempts as well as terrorism. Moreover, Qadhafi's worldwide ambitions—which strongly resemble those of the U.S.S.R. and certain of its close allies—have brought Libyan agents and money to terrorist operations in the Caribbean, Central America, New Zealand, and even the South Pacific island of New Caledonia. At present, the greatest Libyan threat is to the moderate and black states of Africa—mostly Tunisia, Algiers, Egypt, Sudan, Chad, and others further south. The United States is working with these states to help them resist Libyan aggressive plans.

The targets of Middle East terrorism fall principally into four groups: Israel; Western governments and citizens, particularly France and the United States; moderate Arab governments and officials, including the mainline PLO as well as Jordan, Egypt, Kuwait, and Saudi Arabia; and critics of radical regimes, particularly Libyans, who are targeted by their own governments.

While the Middle East might be the source of most terrorism, Europe is the location of the largest number of incidents, ranging from 36% to 53% of the total during each of the past 5 years. Nearly 25% of these incidents, however, are of Middle Eastern origin. Indigenous European terrorists consist of:

• Elements of ethnic groups, such as Corsicans, Basques, Croatians, and Armenians, which have been fighting for autonomy or to redress reputed grievances; in particular, the Armenian groups which have waged a deadly and relentless campaign, both here in the United States and in Europe, against Turkish interests in an effort to establish an Armenian state.

• Leftist groups such as the Red Brigades in Italy, Direct Action in France, Red Army Faction in Germany, the CCC [French acronym for Fighting Communist Cells] in Belgium, Grapo in Spain, and November 17 in Greece.

• Special note should be made of the Provisional Irish Republican Army, the PIRA, which is both ethnic and leftist. It is the most deadly of all European groups, having killed some 50 people in 1984. This group should be distinguished from the IRA of earlier days.

For many years these groups pursued their separate targets independent of each other, but a new phenomenon developed during late 1984 among some of the European leftist groups. Aside from an apparent increase in mutual logistical and propaganda support, groups in Germany, Belgium, and France all attacked NATO-related targets over a period of several months. This resurgence accounted for most of the increase in the total number of incidents in Europe during the past year. There was a lull at the end of the hunger strike by jailed terrorists in Germany, followed by a rash of incidents preceding the annual summit meeting in Bonn. Experts expect that we will see similar outbreaks during future months.

Latin America is the third great center of terrorist incidents, accounting for approximately 20% of the events worldwide. Social, economic, and political turmoil have served to prolong existing patterns of insurgency, which have assumed terrorist dimensions in some countries—particularly Colombia, El Salvador, Guatemala, and Peru. There has been some spillover into Latin America from terrorism in the Middle East and Europe, particularly Iran and Libya. Cuba and Nicaragua provide the strongest encouragement and direct support for terrorist activities in other Latin American countries, particularly those with insurgency situations. They, of course, receive support from the Soviet bloc. In addition, Italian and possibly other leftist terrorists have found refuge in Nicaragua.

U.S. Actions

What is the United States doing to defend itself and its citizens abroad, unilaterally and in cooperation with other governments? Has this been, will it be successful? Given the current preoccupation with the use of force to counter terrorism and the controversy over the lack of U.S. military retaliation to terrorist acts, it may surprise you to learn that there have been successes.

We have identified over 90 planned attacks upon U.S. citizens or facilities abroad during the past year which we are satisfied have been preempted by improved intelligence, stronger security, and cooperation from other governments. There are unconfirmed reports of additional incidents which may have been planned against the United States, but they are not counted because we are uncertain of their validity. There are undoubtedly other incidents of which we are completely unaware. But only terrorist successes receive public attention, leaving the impression that they are all powerful and always successful. Obviously we cannot divulge too much about our successes and about where and why the terrorists failed. This would give the enemy our game plan and the means to overcome our defenses. However, there are several illustrative incidents from the 90 successful cases which can be cited:

- Last fall, the Italian Government prevented a group of Shi'a terrorists from blowing up our Embassy in Rome and arrested the terrorists.

- Our Ambassador and Embassy in Colombia avoided several specific terrorist attacks, including a bomb attack which was stopped short of the Embassy and several bombs destined for U.S. business concerns.

- We have preempted several specific plans to bomb the Embassy residence in Beirut and assassinate or kidnap the Ambassador and other senior officials.

- We detected and defused a large car bomb which would have caused dozens of casualties at a U.S. and NATO training facility in Oberammergau, West Germany.

- The United Kingdom avoided a series of Brighton-type bombings and arrested 14 IRA terrorists in June.

To improve security of diplomatic installations, a new approach was set in motion after the 1983 bombings in Beirut and funded by Congress last fall. Some $55 million has been spent to enhance physical and operational security of our diplomatic posts abroad in the past year. In fiscal years (FY) 1986 and 1987, budget requests for overall security resources total $391 million and $331 million respectively. The number of professional State Department security officers abroad will double during the 1985–86 period and the marine security guard complement has been augmented. Seventy major perimeter security enhancement projects are scheduled for FY 85–86, and a dozen new Embassies are being built to replace those in high-threat countries which are far below acceptable standards. New turnkey procedures involving joint action by the Department of State and private business have been adopted in order to cut completion time to one-third of what it once was.

The Inman panel, headed by Admiral Robert Inman, the former Deputy Director of the CIA, recently proposed a large expansion of the Embassy security program. For the 1986 fiscal year, six specific areas are highlighted for increased security enhancement. These are:

• Construction, relocation, and renovation of scores of buildings that will meet new physical and technical security standards;

• Residential security (to include guard services and field support);

• Perimeter security program;

• Technical countermeasures and counterintelligence programs;

• Foreign Service security training (security training development, overseas guard and post security officer, general security, Federal law enforcement, coping with violence abroad, and firearms and evasive driving); and

• Protective security resources, additional personnel.

Other Developments

It is important to note that in countering terrorism abroad the United States is limited in what it can do alone because we must rely very heavily upon the cooperation of foreign governments who control the countries from which the terrorists come and those in which they operate. We are working hard to increase this cooperation and have made progress. But much more remains to be done.

• The recent series of hijackings, aircraft and airport bombings, as well as the attacks against targets in Western Europe associated with the NATO alliance, has spurred moves toward greater cooperation with our European allies. We are working with friendly countries in Europe and elsewhere to improve sharing of information and techniques in dealing with terrorists.

• In Latin America, progress has also been made, although the travel threat remains very high. For example, during the past year, a coordinated interagency counterterrorist program in Colombia has helped that government regain the initiative from the terrorists and narcotics traffickers.

We will soon be requesting funds urgently for a similar but larger Administration counterterrorism program for Central America. The threat there is becoming more serious. For example, in El Salvador, the guerrillas and terrorists have decided to move into the cities, reacting to successes of U.S.-supported counterinsurgency programs in rural areas. As the assassinations of the American marines and the kidnaping of President Duarte's daughter have indicated, the same trend is likely to continue. This means that the police, who have been getting almost no assistance and are in poor shape, must bear the burden of defending their governments—and U.S. personnel—from terrorist attack. It is essential that Congress act to approve the Administration request for carefully controlled counterterrorist assistance to Central American police forces, administered by the State Department and coordinated with military programs administered by the Defense Department.

• In the Middle East, we will continue our efforts to release the seven Americans still held hostage by Iranian-supported Shi'a terrorists. We will also continue to work with Israel, Jordan, Egypt, and the moderate states of the gulf in opposing terrorism as well as helping them face the threat of conventional attack instigated by Libya, Iran or Syria. We will not change our policies, give up on the peace process, or be driven out of the region, despite the threats to U.S. facilities and citizens.

• In the civil aviation field, the Departments of State and Transportation have taken several important steps, unilaterally and with other governments, to improve security. These include air marshalls, better security screening at U.S. airports and for U.S. airlines abroad, and pressure on other governments to tighten their own security. We are also providing training and technical assistance to some 20 governments in this field. We will not hesitate to act, as we did with Greece and Lebanon, where foreign governments refuse to provide adequate security.

Training Cooperation

Since most terrorism takes place abroad, it is obvious that cooperation with other governments is extremely important in combating this menace. We work on this in many different ways, from publicized, top-level meetings between chiefs of state to unpublicized liaison contacts between the CIA [Central Intelligence Agency] and FBI and services of other governments. The Anti-Terrorism Assistance (ATA) Program has been in operation for only 16 months but is paying big dividends in improved cooperation and support from foreign governments. In the past year we have held high-level, interagency policy consultations on how better to combat terrorism and how to improve bilateral cooperation with a range of governments such as the United Kingdom, Italy, Israel, Egypt, Turkey, Greece, Colombia, Honduras, and Denmark. India and Pakistan, the Netherlands, and France are among those planning to participate. The ATA Program provides training for foreign, civilian law enforcement agencies, focusing upon such fields as civil aviation and airport security, bomb detection and disposal, and hostage negotiation and rescue. Metropolitan police forces in such cities as New York, Los Angeles, Boston, Washington, D.C., Miami, and Chicago have participated, as well as numerous law enforcement organizations. By January 1, 1986, the program will have had almost 2,000 participants from 32 countries.

We also are increasing cooperation with American businesses operating overseas. The Threat Analysis Group of the Office of Security in Washington and the regional security officers at posts overseas encourage contact with the private sector on security issues. The Secretary announced in February the formation of the Overseas Security Advisory Council. It is now operating to bring public sector and private sector officials together to exchange information on security issues and make recommendations for closer operational cooperation.

We continue to explore and develop a number of other multilateral, bilateral, and unilateral options, including the potential use of military force. Secretary of State Shultz has been foremost among those who have said that we need to consider the use of military tools when appropriate. Each terrorist event presents a different situation, however, and while our military forces have been in a high state of readiness in recent crises, the situation has not been appropriate to their actual employment. We must be and we are willing to use force, carefully, if the circumstances call for it.

Although sometimes the media seems to assume that the use of U.S. military force for retaliation is the only means to fight terrorists, this is usually not the case. We and other governments have made preventive strikes through police action—arresting terrorists before they can attack, as was done in Rome. And as we recently saw in El Salvador, where effective action has been taken against some of those responsible for killing American servicemen and civilians in June, military action does not necessarily require the use of American forces. That is one reason why we place so much emphasis upon military and police training and assistance programs for other countries and on closer intelligence and law enforcement cooperation with them.

Conclusion

This overview is by no means the complete story of international terrorism. Books have been written on this subject, and more will be. The same goes for TV. But, I hope it has been useful. On closing, it is important to keep a few things clearly in mind.

The United States must not take a defeatist attitude toward international terrorism. We can make and are making progress. But it will be long and difficult; it takes a great deal of effort and requires cooperation by other nations; and there will be occasional incidents, because the United States is the number one target.

It also is costly. There are costs of improving the physical security of our Embassies and other installations overseas. Private business must also increase expenditures for security, at home and abroad. Using economic pressures or not shipping arms has an impact on governments such as Libya and Iran and others who support terrorism, although it may result in financial pain to individual companies who hope to make lucrative sales.

But we must not and will not retreat, close our military bases, abandon our businesses, change our policies, let down our allies, because of terrorist threats and attacks. That would be much more costly, economically as well as in political and strategic coin. It would also lead to still more terrorism.

Terrorism, as many experts have said, is a form of low-intensity warfare. It is not an easy one to fight. There are no magic weapons—there are no quick fixes. However, I assure you that we are in the struggle for the duration. With your support and that of other sectors of the American public, we will continue to make progress, and the chances for still more success will continue to improve.

THE POWER OF THE FANATICS[3]

People often ask me what was the most frightening moment I lived through in my four years in Lebanon. I saw many grotesque scenes in that country, and was shot at by anonymous madmen more times than I care to remember. But in the end it wasn't the sight or threat of death that scared me most. No, my most frightening moment came at the bar of the Commodore Hotel around lunchtime last Feb. 8.

That was the day after the Shiite Moslem Amal militia had seized control of West Beirut from the Lebanese Army, and groups of Moslem militiamen belonging to the fanatical, pro-Iranian Hizbullah, or "Party of God," had gone on a rampage, ransacking "heathen" bars and houses of prostitution. I was sitting in the hotel restaurant when I heard a ruckus coming from the lobby. I turned around and saw a tall, heavyset Shiite militiaman with a black beard, a wild look in his eye and an M-16 in his hands, heading for the bar.

Expecting such a visit, the bartender had hidden all the liquor bottles under the counter and had replaced them with Pepsi-Cola and Perrier. The militiaman wasn't fooled. He stalked behind the bar, shoved the bartender aside and began smashing every liquor bottle and glass with his rifle butt. When he was done, he strode out of the lobby, leaving behind a small lake of liquor on the floor.

[3]Reprint of an article by Thomas L. Friedman, the *New York Times* bureau chief in Jerusalem. *New York Times*. p 22+. O. 7, '84. Copyright © 1984 by The New York Times Company. Reprinted by permission.

I think the reason the incident was so profoundly disturbing to me was that I confronted that day something I had never seen so close up before—the face of violent religious extremism. That militiaman could just as easily have been smashing human beings as bottles. I don't think it would have made a dime's bit of difference to him. He was from the Party of God, he had truth with a capital T, he had his M-16, and he was not about to let anything stand in his way. He seemed so strong, and we seemed so weak, and that was what was so frightening.

For the first time, I wasn't simply some objective reporter chronicling someone else's misery. It was *my* house that had been invaded, it was *my* liberty that was at stake, and suddenly I had an inkling of what it was like to be the victim of all the extremist violence I had covered. It wasn't like being caught out in the street while some crazy man started shelling your neighborhood from five miles away. This was aimed at me. I saw that militiaman's face, I saw the wild look in his eyes, and I saw how easily he imposed his values on me.

In the coming months, that scene at the Commodore—the lone militiaman breaking up that bar while we stood by and watched, unwilling or unable to defend our way of life—came to symbolize for me the power that is created when political or religious extremism is wedded to violence. I felt as though I had seen moderation and tolerance on the run that afternoon. I felt as though I saw it get up off a barstool and slink away.

More and more, it seems that the political center in both the Arab world and Israel is being hijacked by extremists determined to go to any lengths to pursue their causes. The lethal car bombing of the new American Embassy in Beirut Sept. 20—a numbing reprise of the carnage visited upon the American Marine headquarters and the old embassy last year—is only the latest in an ugly series of extremist actions that have buffeted the Middle East in the last five years. The siege of the Grand Mosque in Mecca by Moslem fanatics, the sponsoring of death squads by Libyan leader Muammar el-Qaddafi, the massacres in Lebanon and Syria, the maiming of West Bank mayors by Jewish terrorists, the utterly ruthless repression of religious and political opponents in the Ayatollah Khomeini's Iran—these are almost the chapter headings of the recent history of the region.

Although political moderates probably remain a majority in the Middle East, they are finding it increasingly difficult to defend their values. My overwhelming impression is that, throughout the area, the moderates are on the run.

I saw moderation on the run in the recent Israeli election campaign, when Rabbi Meir Kahane, an anti-Arab racist, was able to win a seat in the Israeli Knesset, while his ideological opposite, Lova Eliav, who campaigned on a one-man ticket calling for peaceful coexistence with the Arabs, fell far short of the minimum number of votes needed to secure a parliamentary seat.

I saw tolerance smothered on a Friday afternoon in June 1982, when I came home to my Beirut apartment house to find that it had been demolished. Two groups of Palestinian refugees had gotten into a fight over who would take over the eight-story building, and the group that lost simply blew up the whole place, killing my Palestinian driver's wife and two daughters, who happened to be inside my apartment at the time. I will always remember my driver, Muhammed, sitting in the back of a fire-truck, weeping and repeating to himself: "It isn't fair, I am a man of peace, I never carried a gun in my life."

I saw moderation murdered at the American University of Beirut one morning last January, when some so-called revolutionaries pumped two bullets into the head of the university's president, Malcolm Kerr, while he was armed with a briefcase and an umbrella. Malcolm was a man who had dedicated his life to fostering American understanding of Islam and Arab society. The moderate center truly lost a great man in his death.

I saw moderation on the run on May 6, 1984—the day a group of Lebanese peace activists had planned to bring together the silent majority of nonviolent Moslems and Christians for a peace march on the "Green Line" that divided Beirut into hostile camps. When the rival militias got wind of the peace march, they began fighting shortly before the event was scheduled to start. After 22 people were killed and another 130 wounded, the organizers of the demonstration called it off. I will never forget, though, how a tiny group of those Beirut peace activists gathered at the Green Line, despite the danger, in order to remove the marble plaque they had erected there. The plaque said, "Yes to Life, No to War," and they carried it away as though it were a corpse.

These are but a few examples. I could go on. The question is: Why is this happening? Why is it that those who hold the most extreme, the most hard-line, the most uncompromising positions in the Middle East seem so strong of late? What is the source of their strength, and why do they seem to be setting the agenda for us all?

The first reason the extremists are winning is very simple: They are ready to go all the way and use whatever amount of force is necessary to further their causes. In the Middle East, crime pays, and absolute crime pays absolutely. If you are ready to use violence to its ultimate degree, you will not go to jail, you might collect $200, and you may well be elected president. I learned that lesson in the Syrian city of Hama.

Back in February 1982, the regime of Syrian President Hafez al-Assad had a little problem in Hama. It seemed that about 200 of its 180,000 inhabitants belonged to an underground organization known as the Moslem Brotherhood and were trying to organize a rebellion. To make sure that the revolt was quashed, the Government pounded Hama for almost three weeks with tank artillery fire, killing an estimated 20,000 people.

I went to Hama 10 weeks afterward, when the city was reopened to foreigners. I have seen many scenes of destruction in the Middle East, but never anything like Hama. Whole neighborhoods had been plowed up like cornfields and bulldozed as flat as parking lots. Seeing a stoop-shouldered old man with a checkered headdress shuffling along a stretch of rubble the size of four football fields, I asked him where all the houses were.

"You are standing on them," he said.

And where, I asked, were all the people who used to live there?

"You are probably standing on them, too," he answered, shuffling away.

When I kicked the ground, I would unearth a tennis shoe, a tattered photo, a piece of shirt.

The Assad regime had wanted to send a message to Hama—and the rest of Syria—about what would happen to those who tried to challenge its leadership, and the message got through. There has been no anti-Government activity in Syria since.

It is not only in internal affairs that the Syrian Government has elevated extremist violence to an instrument of state. During 1980 and 1981, Syrian agents went on the offensive in Beirut, shooting and killing several Lebanese and Western journalists in order to discourage reporters from writing negatively about Syria. As a member of the press corps at the time, I can testify that the campaign had its intended effect. Although unflattering stories about Syria still got out, there wasn't a journalist in Beirut who didn't think twice, or even three times, about writing ill of the Syrian regime.

The first reason, then, that the extremists are winning in the Middle East is that they are ready to play by their own rules, and their own rules are Hama rules, and Hama rules mean everything goes. The moderate's dilemma is that he cannot defend himself against such violence without becoming just as ugly as his opponents. The result is that while the extremists are going all the way, the moderates tend to just go away.

What I saw while living in Beirut was that the best people, the most sensitive, honest and politically tolerant people, tend not to stand and fight for their way of life. They just don't know how. Rather, they do what moderates everywhere do best—yield to the militants and activists. West Beirut was the perfect example. It had been a unique island of tolerance and cosmopolitanism, where Christians, Moslems and Druse lived side by side. But as pressure from religious extremists grew, the silent, peaceful majority that could afford to leave just picked up and left.

The same process has occurred in Iran, where the Khomeini regime is alleged to have executed thousands of Iranians and has prompted countless others to take flight, and it may be under way in other countries of the Middle East.

But you don't have to smash up a bar or wipe out a city to get your way. Some of the most successful extremists have probably never wielded a gun. But they do know how to wield words, which brings me to my second point.

Extremists, and all those in the Middle East who reject compromise solutions, are gaining strength today because they understand much better than the moderates the importance of language

and agendas. They recognize much more clearly than their opponents that determining how people describe their world, how they see their alternatives, is where the real power lies.

For instance, after the Six-Day War of 1967, elements from the extreme nationalist Israeli movement Gush Emunim were able to generate enough pressure on a succession of hesitant and divided Israeli Cabinets to get the biblical names of Judea and Samaria imposed officially on the territory known in modern times as the West Bank. The new names, repeated in all Israeli radio and television broadcasts and in all Government documents, naturally carried over into the daily language of politics—to such an extent that, during the recent election campaign, even the Labor Party leader, Shimon Peres, referred to the territory as Judea and Samaria.

The Gush Emunim people know that to name something is to own it. They know that any Israeli who calls the area Judea and Samaria can never really deny the argument that this territory is the biblical cradle of Judaism; that, hence, it is Jewish land, and that to return it to Arab sovereignty would involve a kind of sacrilege. To call it the West Bank has much more neutral overtones and leaves open the possibility of compromise.

One can see the battle over language being played out now in the Israeli media: how to describe the 27 Jewish men who were arrested for alleged involvement in violent acts against West Bank Arabs. Some Israeli newspapers describe them as "Jewish terrorists," implying condemnation of the crimes they are accused of. But the defendants' supporters among the Jewish settlers in the West Bank refer to them as the "Jewish underground," a term that evokes images of the underground that fought for Israel's independence in the 1930's and 1940's. The state-run Israeli radio has also come to refer to the 27 men as members of "the underground," and the term seems to be gaining currency.

The ultranationalist forces in Israel that reject any form of territorial compromise with the Arabs have also dominated the debate about the future of the West Bank. They have succeeded in persuading most Israelis that their choice on the West Bank is between the creation of a radical, pro-Soviet Palestinian state and the supposed security of the status quo. The other alternatives, including federation with Jordan, have been written out of the debate.

Imagine how different the debate might be if the agenda were shaped differently—if, for instance, the debate were over the ultimate character of Israel. The choice then would be between whether Israel should absorb one million hostile Palestinian Arabs and eventually lose its Jewish character, or whether Israel should find a safe way to divest itself of the West Bank and retain its Jewish character. As a Peace Now activist said to me, that would be a much better field for debate, but it is not the field the Israeli moderates are fighting on, which is one reason they are on the run.

The same situation holds true in the Arab world. The Arab extremists have imposed an agenda defining as treasonous any Arab accommodation with Israel that contradicts the objective of establishing a Palestinian state in "all" of Palestine. But imagine how different the position of Palestinian moderates would be if they had been able to convince Palestinians that the question on the agenda was not how to get back "everything" but "how to relieve the homelessness of our people and satisfy our minimal demands for national self-determination." Approaching the future with that agenda might have led the Palestinian leaders to make some very different choices at critical stages in their recent history.

It could be said, "Who cares what Shimon Peres calls the West Bank? The fact is, he is privately for compromise, and will prove it if given the chance." Or, "Who cares what the P.L.O. board of directors forces Arafat to say in public? When push comes to shove, it is his private intentions that will matter."

It doesn't always work that way. I learned that covering the April 1983 talks in Amman between Arafat and King Hussein on the subject of the Reagan Plan for some form of federation between the West Bank and Jordan. There was no question that Arafat wanted to go along with the Jordanian monarch and agree to negotiations on the American President's proposal. But when Arafat flew to Kuwait to convince the P.L.O. central committee members of the wisdom of going along with some form of the Reagan initiative, they overwhelmingly rejected his arguments.

The fault lay squarely with Arafat. After all those years of talking out of both sides of his mouth, after all those years of using the language of extremism in public and the language of moderation in private, Arafat had abandoned the public debate to his hard-line rivals. When the time came for him to marshal a constituency for compromise within his own movement, the support was not there. He had never shaped it.

Arafat had always treated his public statements as mere words, which he could manipulate any way he wanted. But, in the end, he became a prisoner of those words. When Arafat presented his case for going with King Hussein, his hard-line colleagues did not understand the words coming out of his mouth. You can almost imagine what they must have said to him: "What do you mean, go along with the Reagan Plan. Why, we rejected that at the Palestine National Council. You yourself declared that it was not enough, you yourself agreed to the final statement condemning it." In saving his moderation for visiting European dignitaries and Western correspondents, Arafat had not prepared the ground for compromise within his own movement.

Political extremists and religious fanatics understand the importance not only of language and agenda but of simplicity. That brings me to the third reason why extremists are winning. They are willing and able to simplify their positions into short clichés that divert attention from the complexities and constraints of the real world. Extremists have always been much better at exploiting the media, understanding as they do that the media responds to simplicity, to black and white.

One of the founders of Peace Now was explaining to me in Jerusalem recently the difficulty he had in defending his position on the West Bank in public debate with, for example, some of the more extreme followers of Gush Emunim. "When you ask the Gush Emunim people why Israel should keep the West Bank," he said, "they have a very simple answer, only two words—'It's ours.'" What Jew can deny that it was on the West Bank that the heart of the ancient Jewish kingdom was located? But, as the Peace Now activist conceded, when he is asked for his view of the issue, he gives a five-page position paper about long-term demographics, and the decline of humanistic values, and so on and so on, a reply that does not stand a chance against a two-word answer.

Palestinian moderates have the same problem. Palestinian hard-liners have a clear and simple answer when they are asked why they will not settle for half of Palestine, instead of demanding all of it. Their answer is three words: "It's *all* ours." Historically speaking, what Palestinian can argue with that? If you ask dovish Palestinians, like the late Issam Sartawi, why they think the Palestinians should agree to a compromise, they will give you a long, guarded explanation why half a loaf is better than no loaf at all, and all the time they will be looking over their shoulder for the assassin's bullet. Unfortunately for Sartawi, that bullet eventually caught up with him.

I am sure that, deep down, some of the extremists, on both the Palestinian and the Jewish side, know that their two-word answers do not do justice to the issues involved. But they are not out to do justice. They are out to advance their beliefs and interests, and, by shamelessly simplifying everything, they have been quite effective.

In the recent Israeli election campaign, extreme right-wing opponents of the Labor Party printed some advertisements depicting Shimon Peres as the whitest of doves. One ad had pictures of Arafat, Bethlehem Mayor Elias Freij, former Austrian Chancellor Bruno Kreisky and Ahmed Jabril, the leader of a radical, pro-Syrian P.L.O. faction. The message under the pictures asked what all those men had in common and gave an answer: "They all want the Labor Party to win." The fact that there were enormous differences between a man like Freij, who supported coexistence between Israel and the Palestinians, and Jabril, a Syrian puppet who rejected any kind of coexistence and was Freij's sworn enemy, was ignored.

Not surprisingly, one found Arafat engaging in the same form of verbal extremism. When the Labor Party beat Likud in the recent Israeli elections, Arafat told a Kuwaiti newspaper, "It was just a snake changing its skin."

It would be convenient to dismiss these Israeli ads and Arafat statements as so much political hyperbole, but I believe they do matter. They matter because when people do not make distinc-

ing quiet satisfaction that the "Pharaoh," as they called Sadat, was dead. His economic policies and his family's ostentatious life style had alienated him from many of his people, and the men who killed him were expressing violently a very popular sentiment in their country.

I remember talking to a hotel desk clerk who told me about a wedding party that had been scheduled at her hotel only a few hours after Sadat was gunned down, and how the celebration went ahead as though nothing unpleasant had happened. A friend of mine who returned from Egypt recently told me that in walking around Cairo, he had had a hard time finding pictures of Sadat in any public place.

Similarly, anyone who says the Jewish terrorists in Israel are a fringe element is fooling himself, and there are polls that make this clear. One poll, taken by the newspaper Ha'aretz after the 27 men were arrested, found that 31.8 percent of the Israeli public regarded the terrorists' actions as either fully or partly justified. It was revealed in the court papers that, in some instances, when the terrorist ringleaders visited a Jewish house to recruit a new member and the person they came to see was out, they would make their appeal to whoever was home. The image of secret underground meetings in caves by candlelight does not apply.

An Israeli friend of mine told me of a discussion he had with his maid about the Jewish terrorists; he asked her what she thought of them. The woman, whose family had emigrated from the Jewish community of Morocco, said it was terrible that they had been arrested. After all, she said, it wasn't fair that the Arabs should be able to have an underground and the Jews not. The sentiment may be simple, but it has an intuitive appeal to a substantial portion of the Israeli public.

Perhaps, then, what is most worrisome about such developments in the Middle East is not the rise of the extremist fringe but the rise of an extremist center. As extremist violence engulfs more and more people's lives, it gains more and more recruits. Behind every extremist act, one can usually find an amorphous body of feelings and attitudes that supports it to a significant degree.

Which leads to the fifth and final reason that extremism is gaining strength. It feeds on itself, and it feeds on frustration, and it feeds on insensitivity, and right now there is a glut of all three in the Middle East.

The Arab world, in particular, is going through a frustrating era. There is an ideological vacuum, a gnawing feeling that all the political solutions have been tried and none of them have worked. The old ideologies, from Nasserism to Arab Socialism, have proved to be bankrupt and incapable of solving the fundamental political, social and economic problems of Arab societies, let alone redressing their basic weakness, compared to Israel. The expectations of the early 1970's that oil wealth would enable the Arab world to transform itself have been dashed. This has produced cynicism and a sense of impotence, and has created a wide opening for frustration. In many cases, this void has been filled by extreme religious fundamentalism offering a messianic solution that secular politics has failed to deliver.

There is another dynamic to extremism. In feeding on itself, it sets off a chain reaction that is felt around the region. Witness the phenomenon of Rabbi Kahane. During the recent Israeli election campaign, Kahane's advertisements were very simple. He would stand in front of a television camera and declare with a snarl, "Give me your votes, and I will take care of *them*." "Them," of course, were Israel's Arab citizens. When he won a seat in Parliament, it was the most talked-about result of the election. "How could this happen?" people asked. "Who could have elected such a xenophobic extremist?"

Who elected Meir Kahane? The Arabs, I believe. The votes may have been Jewish, but the conditions for his success were created largely by the Arab states. By refusing to recognize Israel and negotiate with it directly, the Arabs have only strengthened Israeli fanatics like Rabbi Kahane, enabling them to play on the legitimate fears and security concerns of the Israeli public. The Arabs have always deluded themselves into believing that they would get what they wanted out of Israel by organizing pressure against it from the outside. But the road to a Palestinian homeland does not run through United Nations resolutions, or hijackings, or even warfare. It runs through the Israeli public and Israeli democracy.

There is still a majority for compromise in Israel, but it has to be activated through dialogue and recognition. It is only the Arabs, I believe, who can bring Kahane down—by negotiating with Israel on a political settlement.

As for the link between extremism and insensitivity, look at the garden of fanaticism the Israelis have been cultivating in southern Lebanon, whose population is roughly 80 percent Shiite Moslem and 20 percent Christian. From almost the day the Israeli Army invaded the area, its policy has been a chronicle of insensitivity and error. This has created an extremist Shiite opposition among people who only two years earlier greeted the Israelis with rice and flowers as their liberators from the capricious rule of the P.L.O. Instead of seeking to work quietly through the legitimate Shiite leadership in the south, represented by the Amal militia, the Israelis imposed Maj. Saad Haddad, a Greek Orthodox Christian, as their effective governor general of the whole region—a serious affront to the Shiites, who probably could have served just as effectively as an anti-P.L.O. force.

When the Israelis finally did try enlisting local Shiite support, they tended to favor the traditional landowning families, which had long ago lost their popular power bases. The Israelis made their most serious blunder on Oct. 16, 1983, when one of their patrols tried to drive through a crowd of 50,000 Shiites in the village of Nabiteyeh, who were commemorating the most holy day of their calendar, Ashura. This precipitated a riot that left two Shiites dead, 15 wounded, and thousands embittered. The Israeli soldiers were later disciplined, but not before the damage had been done.

The end result of all of this is that the Shiites of southern Lebanon have become the sworn enemies of Israel as much as of the P.L.O. Their opposition to Israel is being organized in the mosques, and is increasingly taking on the extremist overtones of Islam against Judaism. A day rarely goes by anymore without sniper fire, booby-trap bombs or grenades being directed against Israeli soldiers. The more the Israelis try to protect themselves by blocking traffic, checking cars and searching homes, the more they antagonize the local population.

Given the increasing velocity of extremist violence in the Middle East, one might well ask whether there is any hope for moderate solutions to the problems of the region. When I need a dose of optimism, I think about Moshe Dayan and Sharm el-Sheikh.

For years, the Israeli general and war hero would declare, "Better Israel should not have peace with Egypt and keep Sharm el-Sheikh than give up Sharm el-Sheikh and have peace with Egypt." Sharm el-Sheikh, it may be recalled, was the little base at the southern tip of the Sinai Peninsula that General Dayan thought was more important to Israel's survival than peace with its strongest Arab enemy.

Then Sadat came to Israel. He extended his hand in friendship, and Moshe Dayan discovered things in himself and in his former enemy that he never knew were there. Suddenly, the world looked different to him. Suddenly, he had a completely different agenda. Suddenly, Sharm el-Sheikh looked very small.

There is a very important lesson here. We have an enormous power to shape each other, and when you create a new dynamic between people, all kinds of new things become possible.

People I meet often say to me, "You've talked to Yasir Arafat. Tell me, is he really a moderate?" I always have the same answer: "I don't know, and, more important, Yasir Arafat doesn't know. And he will not know until he is tested." It took Anwar Sadat to bring out the moderate in Moshe Dayan and Menachem Begin, and it will take some Israeli to bring out the moderate in Yasir Arafat. And it will take an overture by Arafat to bring out the moderate in many Israelis. But, as Sadat showed, people can change; stereotypes can crumble.

But Sadat is dead, the spirit of his initiative has faded, and in my darker moments I fear that Lebanon is the future, a harbinger of things to come throughout the Middle East. Nine years of civil war, fear, greed and selfishness have driven every Lebanese religious community to its most extreme position. The values of tolerance and compromise disappeared long ago from the local vocabulary. Politics in Lebanon, in fact, is simply the politics of competing extremes, and I wonder if this trend is not spreading to the region as a whole.

Of the many horrific scenes I took away from Beirut, there is one in particular that I will never forget. It took place in Shatila a few days after the massacre. The Red Cross workers had come into the camp, had collected the bodies and were burying them in a mass grave in an empty field. They had dug a long, 12-foot-deep trench and were carrying the bodies down there, one by one. They would lay out a row of bodies, pour white lime over them to deaden the stench, and cover them with dirt. Then they would put another layer on top of these, and so on, until the grave was filled.

As I stood watching, I noticed, next to me, a little Palestinian boy. He was wearing a red shirt and shorts, and was sitting on a small stool. He could not have been more than 8 or 9 years old, and I remember he had a white gauze mask to fend off the stench, but it was too large for him and had fallen down around his neck. His eyes were full of tears. He was obviously watching members of his own family being buried, maybe his entire family for all I know.

I remember looking at that little boy and thinking that no one, let alone a child, should ever have to watch such a wretched scene as this burial. I remember wondering what lifelong scars were being formed right then and there on that boy's mind, what desire for revenge was being planted in his heart.

This is how it happens, I thought to myself. This is how the cycle keeps going. One generation watches another go to its miserable, miserable grave, and a new generation of avengers, of extremists, of people unable to make distinctions, is born.

What I hope is that the lesson of Anwar Sadat's initiative and Moshe Dayan's response will be learned before too long, and save that little boy from his destiny as another hate-filled extremist. What I fear is that his scars and his passions will win the day and set the agenda for us all.

II. THE INTERNATIONAL CONNECTION

EDITOR'S INTRODUCTION

Within the borders of the United States, terrorism is relatively rare. Armed robberies and murders are occasionally committed by "revolutionaries" like the left-wing Black Liberation Army and the right-wing Aryan Nation, and there have been firebombings of abortion and contraception clinics by antiabortion activists. But, on the whole, Americans at home are more likely to be the target of criminals than of terrorists. (It should be remembered, however, that some forms of terrorism have a long history in the United States. The lynching of blacks by whites was still common in the South well into our own century.)

The problem of international terrorism, on the other hand, grows more acute each year as it becomes evident that the nations most afflicted by terrorism are unwilling or unable to punish their attackers. The lack of cooperation among target nations was given dramatic emphasis in two recent episodes: the hijacking of TWA Flight 847 in June 1985 and the hijacking of the cruise ship *Achille Lauro* in September 1985. In the first, Greece freed a captured accomplice of the hijackers in exchange for the release of Greek hostages aboard the jet. In the second, the hijackers, allowed to go free by Egypt, were intercepted by U.S. forces and flown to Italy. Italy, however, refused to detain the alleged leader of the operation, an act of capitulation that eventually caused the government to fall. With such disunity prevailing among the nations affected by terrorism, it is little wonder that progress against it is slow.

This section opens with remarks, reprinted from the *Department of State Bulletin* and *Vital Speeches of the Day*, by Secretary of State George Shultz and CIA director William J. Casey on the vulnerability of democracies to terrorist attack and the difficulties involved in obtaining information about terrorist groups and convincing democracies to put aside short-term priorities in order to cooperate in their own defense. Both articles make mention of the role of the Soviet Union and radical Islamic states in sponsoring terrorist activities. As Casey says, terrorism is a highly "cost-effective" way for these states to destabilize the democratic nations by playing on their own weaknesses—far more cost-effective than conventional warfare. These issues are developed further in the third selection, a *World Press Review* collection of reports from the Brazilian, Egyptian, West German, and Hong Kong press. One of these, "'Born' in the U.S.," calls attention to the fact that some terrorists receive their training in the United States at paramilitary camps set up to train mercenaries to destabilize Marxist governments in Central America. The vast majority of international terrorists, however, receive arms, training, and financial support from the USSR and its client states and from Libya, Syria, and Iran. The motives and activities of Libya's leader, Muammar el-Qaddafi, are examined in the last selection, an article from *Newsweek* magazine.

TERRORISM: THE CHALLENGE TO THE DEMOCRACIES[1]

Five years have passed since the Jonathan Institute held its first conference on terrorism, and in that time the world has seen two major developments: one a cause for great distress; the other a reason for hope.

The distressing fact is that over these past 5 years terrorism has increased. More people were killed or injured by international terrorists last year than in any year since governments began keeping records. In 1983 there were more than 500 such attacks, of which more than 200 were against the United States. For Americans the worst tragedies were the destruction of our Embassy and then the Marine barracks in Beirut. But around the world, many

[1]Address by Secretary of State George Shultz before the Jonathan Institute's second Conference on International Terrorism, June 24, 1984. *Department of State Bulletin.* 84:31–4. Ag. '84.

of our close friends and allies were also victims. The bombing of Harrods in London, the bombing at Orly Airport in Paris, the destruction of a Gulf Air flight in the United Arab Emirates, and the Rangoon bombing of South Korean officials are just a few examples—not to mention the brutal attack on a West Jerusalem shopping mall this past April.

Even more alarming has been the rise of state-sponsored terrorism. In the past 5 years more states have joined the ranks of what we might call the "League of Terror," as full-fledged sponsors and supporters of indiscriminate—and not so indiscriminate—murder. Terrorist attacks supported by what [Libyan leader] Qadhafi calls the "holy alliance" of Libya, Syria, and Iran, and attacks sponsored by North Korea and others, have taken a heavy toll of innocent lives. Seventy or more such attacks in 1983 probably involved significant state support or participation.

As a result, more of the world's people must today live in fear of sudden and unprovoked violence at the hands of terrorists. After 5 years, the epidemic is spreading and the civilized world is still groping for remedies.

Nevertheless, these past 5 years have also given us cause for hope. Thanks in large measure to the efforts of concerned governments, citizens, and groups like the Jonathan Institute, the peoples of the free world have finally begun to grapple with the problem of terrorism in intellectual and in practical terms. I say intellectual because the first step toward a solution to any problem is to understand that there is a problem and then to understand its nature. In recent years we have learned a great deal about terrorism, though our education has been painful and costly. We know what kind of threat international terrorism poses to our free society. We have learned much about the terrorists themselves, their supporters, their targets, their diverse methods, their underlying motives, and their eventual goals.

Armed with this knowledge we can focus our energies on the practical means for reducing and eventually eliminating the threat. We can all share the hope that, when the next conference of this institute is convened, we will look back and say that 1984 was the turning point in our struggle against terrorism, that having come to grips with the problem we were able to deal with it effectively and responsibly.

The Anatomy of Terrorism

Let me speak briefly about the anatomy of terrorism. What we have learned about terrorism, first of all, is that it is not random, undirected, purposeless violence. It is not, like an earthquake or a hurricane, an act of nature before which we are helpless. Terrorists and those who support them have definite goals; terrorist violence is the means of attaining those goals. Our response must be twofold: we must deny them the means but above all we must deny them their goals.

But what are the goals of terrorism? We know that the phenomenon of terrorism is actually a matrix that covers a diverse array of methods, resources, instruments, and immediate aims. It appears in many shapes and sizes—from the lone individual who plants a homemade explosive in a shopping center, to the small clandestine group that plans kidnapings and assassinations of public figures, to the well-equipped and well-financed organization that uses force to terrorize an entire population. Its stated objectives may range from separatist causes to revenge for ethnic grievances to social and political revolution. International drug smugglers use terrorism to blackmail and intimidate government officials. It is clear that our responses will have to fit the precise character and circumstances of the specific threats.

But we must understand that the overarching goal of all terrorists is the same: with rare exceptions, they are attempting to impose their will by force—a special kind of force designed to create an atmosphere of fear. And their efforts are directed at destroying what all of us here are seeking to build. They're a threat to the democracies.

The Threat to the Democracies

The United States and its democratic allies are morally committed to certain ideals and to a humane vision of the future. In our foreign policies, we try to foster the kind of world that promotes peaceful settlement of disputes, one that welcomes change without violent conflict. We seek a world in which human rights are respected by all governments, a world based on the rule of law.

We know that in a world community where all nations share these blessings, our own democracy will flourish, our own nation will prosper, and our own people will continue to enjoy freedom.

Nor has ours been a fruitless search. In our lifetime, we have seen the world progress, though perhaps too slowly, toward this goal. Civilized norms of conduct have evolved, even governing relations between adversaries. Conflict persists; but, with some notorious exceptions, even wars have been conducted with certain restraints—indiscriminate slaughter of innocents is widely condemned; the use of certain kinds of weapons has been proscribed; and most, but not all, nations have heeded those proscriptions.

We all know that the world as it exists is still far from our ideal vision. But today, even the progress that mankind has already made is endangered by those who do not share that vision—who, indeed, violently oppose it.

For we must understand, above all, that terrorism is a form of political violence. Wherever it takes place, it is directed in an important sense against us, the democracies—against our most basic values and often our fundamental strategic interests. The values upon which democracy is based—individual rights, equality under law, freedom of thought and expression, and freedom of religion—all stand in the way of those who seek to impose their will, their ideologies, or their religious beliefs by force. A terrorist has no patience and no respect for the orderly processes of democratic society, and, therefore, he considers himself its enemy.

And it is an unfortunate irony that the very qualities that make democracies so hateful to the terrorists also make them so vulnerable. Precisely because we maintain the most open societies, terrorists have unparalleled opportunity to strike against us.

Terrorists and Freedom Fighters

The antagonism between democracy and terrorism seems so basic that it is hard to understand why so much intellectual confusion still exists on the subject. We have all heard the insidious claim that "one man's terrorist is another man's freedom fighter." Let me read to you the powerful rebuttal that was stated before your 1979 conference by a great American, Senator Henry Jackson, who, Mr. Chairman, as you observed, is very much with us.

The idea that one person's "terrorist" is another's "freedom fighter" cannot be sanctioned. Freedom fighters or revolutionaries don't blow up buses containing non-combatants; terrorist murderers do. Freedom fighters don't set out to capture and slaughter school children; terrorist murderers do. Freedom fighters don't assassinate innocent businessmen, or hijack and hold hostage innocent men, women, and children; terrorist murderers do. It is a disgrace that democracies would allow the treasured word "freedom" to be associated with acts of terrorists.

Where democracy is struggling to take root, the terrorist is, again, its enemy. He seeks to spread chaos and disorder, to paralyze a society. In doing so he wins no converts to his cause; his deeds inspire hatred and fear, not allegiance. The terrorist seeks to undermine institutions, to destroy popular faith in moderate government, and to shake the people's belief in the very idea of democracy. In Lebanon, for example, state-sponsored terrorism has exploited existing tensions and attempted to prevent that nation from rebuilding its democratic institutions.

Where the terrorist cannot bring about anarchy, he may try to force the government to overreact, or impose tyrannical measures of control, and hence lose the allegiance of the people. Turkey faced such a challenge but succeeded in overcoming it. Martial law was imposed; the terrorist threat was drastically reduced; and today we see democracy returning to that country. In Argentina, the widely and properly deplored "disappearances" of the 1970s were, in fact, part of a response—a deliberately provoked response—to a massive campaign of terrorism. We are pleased that Argentina, too, has returned to the path of democracy. Other countries around the world face similar challenges, and they, too, must steer their course carefully between anarchy and tyranny. The lesson for civilized nations is that we must respond to the terrorist threat within the rule of law, lest we become unwitting accomplices in the terrorist's scheme to undermine civilized society.

Once we understand terrorism's goals and methods, it is not too hard to tell, as we look around the world, who are the terrorists and who are the freedom fighters. The resistance fighters in Afghanistan do not destroy villages or kill the helpless. The *contras* in Nicaragua do not blow up school buses or hold mass executions of civilians.

How tragic it would be if democratic societies so lost confidence in their own moral legitimacy that they lost sight of the obvious: that violence directed against democracy or the hopes for democracy lacks fundamental justification. Democracy offers mechanisms for peaceful change, legitimate political competition, and redress of grievances. But resort to arms in behalf of democracy against repressive regimes or movements is, indeed, a fight for freedom, since there may be no other way that freedom can be achieved.

The free nations cannot afford to let the Orwellian corruption of language hamper our efforts to defend ourselves, our interests, or our friends. We know the difference between terrorists and freedom fighters, and our policies reflect that distinction. Those who strive for freedom and democracy will always have the sympathy and, when possible, the support of the American people. We will oppose guerrilla wars where they threaten to spread totalitarian rule or deny the rights of national independence and self-determination. But we will oppose terrorists no matter what banner thay may fly. For terrorism in any cause is the enemy of freedom.

The Supporters of Terrorism

If freedom and democracy are the targets of terrorism, it is clear that totalitarianism is its ally. The number of terrorist incidents in or against totalitarian states is negligible. States that support and sponsor terrorist actions have managed in recent years to co-opt and manipulate the phenomenon in pursuit of their own strategic goals.

It is not a coincidence that most acts of terrorism occur in areas of importance to the West. More than 80% of the world's terrorist attacks in 1983 occurred in West Europe, Latin America, and the Middle East. The recent posture statement of the Joint Chiefs of Staff put it this way:

Terrorists may or may not be centrally controlled by their patrons. Regardless, the instability they create in the industrialized West and Third World nations undermines the security interests of the United States and its allies.

States that sponsor terrorism are using it as another weapon of warfare, to gain strategic advantage where they cannot use conventional means. When Iran and its allies sent terrorists to bomb Western personnel in Beirut, they hoped to weaken the West's commitment to defending its interests in the Middle East. When North Korea sponsored the murder of South Korean Government officials, it hoped to weaken the noncommunist stronghold on the mainland of East Asia. The terrorists who assault Israel are also enemies of the United States. When Libya and the Palestine Liberation Organization provide arms and training to the communists in Central America, they are aiding Soviet efforts to undermine our security in that vital region. When the Soviet Union and its clients provide financial, logistic, and training support for terrorists worldwide; when the Red Brigades in Italy and the Red Army faction in Germany assault free countries in the name of communist ideology—they hope to shake the West's self-confidence and sap its will to resist aggression and intimidation. And we are now watching the Italian authorities unravel the answer to one of the great questions of our time: was there Soviet-bloc involvement in the attempt to assassinate the Pope?

We should understand the Soviet role in international terrorism without exaggeration or distortion: the Soviet Union officially denounces the use of terrorism as an instrument of state policy. Yet there is a wide gap between Soviet words and Soviet actions. One does not have to believe that the Soviets are puppeteers and the terrorists marionettes; violent or fanatic individuals and groups are indigenous to every society. But in many countries, terrorism would long since have passed away had it not been for significant support from outside. The international links among terrorist groups are now clearly understood; and the Soviet link, direct or indirect, is also clearly understood. The Soviets use terrorist groups for their own purposes, and their goal is always the same—to weaken liberal democracy and undermine world stability.

A Counterstrategy against Terrorism

Having identified the challenge, we must now consider the best strategy to counter it. We must keep in mind, as we devise our strategy, that our ultimate aim is to preserve what the terrorists seek to destroy: democracy, freedom, and the hope for a world at peace.

The battle against terrorism must begin at home. Terrorism has no place in our society, and we have taken vigorous steps to see that it is not imported from abroad. We are now working with the Congress on law enforcement legislation that would help us obtain more information about terrorists through the payment of rewards to informants and would permit prosecution of those who support states that use or sponsor terrorism. Our FBI is improving our ability to detect and prevent terrorist acts within our own borders.

We must also ensure that our people and facilities in other countries are better protected against terrorist attacks. So we are strengthening security at our Embassies around the world to prevent a recurrence of the Beirut and Kuwait Embassy bombings.

While we take these measures to protect our own citizens, we know that terrorism is an international problem that requires the concerted efforts of all free nations. Just as there is collaboration among those who engage in terrorism, so there must be cooperation among those who are its actual and potential targets.

An essential component of our strategy, therefore, has been greater cooperation among the democratic nations and all others who share our hopes for the future. The world community has achieved some successes. But, too often, countries are inhibited by fear of losing commercial opportunities or fear of provoking the bully. The time has come for the nations that truly seek an end to terrorism to join together, in whatever forums, to take the necessary steps. The declaration on terrorism that was agreed upon at the London economic summit 2 weeks ago was a welcome sign that the industrial democracies share a common view of the terrorist threat. And let me say that I trust and I hope that the statement and the specific things referred to in it will be the tip and only the visible part of the iceberg. We must build on that foundation.

Greater international cooperation offers many advantages. If we can collectively improve our gathering and sharing of intelligence, we can better detect the movements of terrorists, anticipate their actions, and bring them to justice. We can also help provide training and share knowledge of terrorist tactics. To that end, the Reagan Administration has acted promptly on the program that Congress approved last year to train foreign law enforcement officers in anti-terrorist techniques. And the President has sent Congress two bills to implement two international conventions to which the United States is a signatory: the International Convention Against the Taking of Hostages and the Montreal convention to protect against sabotage of civilian aircraft.

We must also make a collective effort to address the special problem of state-sponsored terrorism. States that support terror offer safehavens, funds, training, and logistical support. We must do some hard thinking about how to pressure members of the "League of Terror" to cease their support. Such pressure will have to be international, for no one country can exert sufficient influence alone. Economic sanctions and other forms of pressure impose costs on the nations that apply them, but some sacrifices will be necessary if we are to solve the problem. In the long run, I believe, it will have been a small price to pay.

We must also discourage nations from paying blackmail to terrorist organizations. Although we recognize that some nations are particularly vulnerable to the terrorist threat, we must convince them that paying blackmail is counterproductive and inimical to the interests of all.

Finally, the nations of the free world must stand together against terrorism to demonstrate our enduring commitment to our shared vision. The terrorists may be looking for signs of weakness, for evidence of disunity. We must show them that we are unbending. Let the terrorists despair of ever achieving their goals.

Active Defense

All the measures I have described so far, domestic and international, are important elements in a comprehensive strategy. But are they enough? Is the purely passive defense that these measures entail sufficient to cope with the problem? Can we as a country—can the community of free nations—stand in a solely defensive posture and absorb the blows dealt by terrorists?

I think not. From a practical standpoint, a purely passive defense does not provide enough of a deterrent to terrorism and the states that sponsor it. It is time to think long, hard, and seriously about more active means of defense—about defense through appropriate preventive or preemptive actions against terrorist groups before they strike.

We will need to strengthen our capabilities in the area of intelligence and quick reaction. Human intelligence will be particularly important, since our societies demand that we know with reasonable clarity just what we are doing. Experience has taught us over the years that one of the best deterrents to terrorism is the certainty that swift and sure measures will be taken against those who engage in it. As President Reagan has stated:

> We must make it clear to any country that is tempted to use violence to undermine democratic governments, destabilize our friends, thwart efforts to promote democratic governments, or disrupt our lives, that it has nothing to gain, and much to lose.

Clearly there are complicated moral issues here. But there should be no doubt of the democracies' moral right, indeed duty, to defend themselves.

And there should be no doubt of the profound issue at stake. The democracies seek a world order that is based on justice. When innocents are victimized and the guilty go unpunished, the terrorists have succeeded in undermining the very foundation of civilized society, for they have created a world where there is no justice. This is a blow to our most fundamental moral values and a dark cloud over the future of humanity. We can do better than this.

No matter what strategy we pursue, the terrorist threat will not disappear overnight. This is not the last conference that will be held on this subject. We must understand this and be prepared to live with the fact that despite all our best efforts the world is still a dangerous place. Further sacrifices, as in the past, may be the price for preserving our freedom.

It is essential, therefore, that we not allow the actions of terrorists to affect our policies or deflect us from our goals. When terrorism succeeds in intimidating governments into altering their foreign policies, it only opens the door to more terrorism. It shows that terrorism works; it emboldens those who resort to it; and it encourages others to join their ranks.

The Future

If we remain firm, we can look ahead to a time when terrorism will cease to be a major factor in world affairs. But we must face the challenge with realism, determination, and strength of will. Not so long ago we faced a rash of political kidnapings and embassy takeovers. These problems seemed insurmountable. Yet, through increased security and the willingness of governments to resist terrorist demands and to use force when appropriate, such incidents have become rare. In recent years, we have also seen a decline in the number of airline hijackings—once a problem that seemed to fill our newspapers daily. Tougher security measures and closer international cooperation have clearly had their effect.

I have great faith that we do have the will, and the capability, to act decisively against this threat. It is really up to us, the nations of the free world. We must apply ourselves to the task of ensuring our future and consigning terrorism to its own dismal past.

INTERNATIONAL TERRORISM: POTENT CHALLENGE TO AMERICAN INTELLIGENCE[2]

International terrorism has become a pitiless war without borders. This evening I plan to tell you about how the American Intelligence Community assesses this dreadful scourge, and how I think we should deal with it.

In the last few years we have witnessed the bombings of our embassies in Beirut and in Kuwait, suicide attacks on American

[2]Address by William J. Casey, director of the C.I.A., at the Fletcher School of Law and Diplomacy, April 17, 1985. *Vital Speeches of the Day.* 51:713–17. S. 15, '85.

and French forces in Beirut, the North Korean bombing of the South Korean cabinet in Rangoon, the assassinations of President Bashir Gemayel and Prime Minister Indira Gandhi, and the attempted assassinations of Prime Minister Thatcher in Brighton and Pope John Paul II in St. Peter's Square. We are engaged here in a new form of low-intensity warfare against an enemy that is hard to find and harder still to defend against. The number of recorded international terrorist incidents rose from about 500 in 1983 to more than 700 in 1984. Last year 355 international terrorist bombings occurred—nearly one for every day of the entire year.

U.S. citizens and property always have been among the most popular targets of international terrorism. Last year a large number of attacks also were directed at the French, the Jordanians, and the Israelis. While the Middle East remains the most fertile ground for terrorism, there are ominous developments in Western Europe where left-wing terrorist groups combined forces and began tackling NATO targets.

In confronting the challenge of international terrorism, the first step is to call things by their proper names. We must see clearly and say plainly what the terrorists are, who they are, what goals they seek, and which governments support them.

What the terrorist does is to kill, maim, kidnap, and torture. His victims may be children in a schoolroom, innocent travelers on airplanes, businessmen returning home from work, political leaders, diplomats, industrialists, military officers—anyone. The terrorist's victim may have no particular political identity—or they may be highly visible political symbols like Aldo Moro, or perhaps, like Pope John Paul II. They may be kidnapped and held for ransom, or maimed, or simply blown to bits. The defining characteristic of the terrorist, however, is his choice of method. The terrorist invariably chooses violence as the instrument of first resort.

Terrorism once manifested itself in fundamentally different forms than we see today. Earlier in this century we saw forms of terrorism which usually had its roots in ethnic or separatist groups and which confined its activities to a small geographic area and very selective targets. Even today remnants of this brand of terror-

ism still are with us. The Basque separatists in Spain, the Croatian nationalists in Yugoslavia, the Moro tribesmen in the
Philippines, and other ethnic and separatist groups survive.

Since the late 1960s, we have witnessed the rapid development
of a new stripe of terrorism which is primarily urban and, for the
most part, ideological in nature. In Europe, for example, extremist ideology has spawned such urban terrorist groups as the Red
Army Faction in West Germany, the Communist Combatant
Cells in Belgium, the Direct Action in France, and the Red Brigades in Italy. In the Middle East we note several extremist Palestinian groups including some factions of the Palestine Liberation
Organization. In South America, which has been relatively peaceful on the terrorist front for the past decade or so, similar groups
again seem to be maturing after the decline of terrorism in Uruguay and Argentina over a decade ago. New groups are appearing
in countries such as Chile, Colombia, Ecuador, and Peru.

But a major new departure is state-supported terrorism used
as an instrument of foreign policy. And the chief protagonists of
this departure in international murder are Iran and Libya. Probably more blood has been shed by Iranian-sponsored terrorists during the last few years than by all other terrorists combined.
Tehran uses terrorism as a major element of its ongoing campaign
to export the Iranian revolution throughout the Muslim world
and to reduce Western influence—especially that of the United
States—in the Middle East. In 1983 we identified as many as 50
terrorist attacks with a confirmed or suspected Iranian involvement. Most of these incidents occurred in Lebanon where radical
Shias of the Hizballah, or "Party of God," operated with direct
Iranian support from terrorist bases in the Syrian-controlled Bekaa Valley. To protect themselves from direct retribution, they
tried to mask their activities under the nom de plume "Islamic
Jihad," which is sort of an umbrella trade name.

Iranian-sponsored terrorism was the major factor elsewhere
in the Middle East in 1983 as well. Members of the Islamic Call
Party—another Iranian-sponsored group largely coming out of
Iraq—who received training and direction in Tehran, successfully
carried out six bombings on 12 December 1983, including one
blast which damaged the American Embassy in Kuwait. Iran also

continued its active recruitment and training program through Muslim Shi'ite recruiters in the Persian Gulf, Africa, and even Asia. Many of these recruits are today available for subversive or terrorist operations, particularly in the oil-rich Persian Gulf states where pro-Iranian dissidents and Iranian agents are hanging over those small states like the Sword of Damocles.

Most alarming in 1984 was the accumulating evidence that Iranian-sponsored terrorism was increasing in scope and effectiveness in Western Europe. We believe that agents working out of Iranian Embassies and Islamic cultural or student centers in several European nations will continue to attempt operations in Western Europe in the near future.

Although Libya's Qadhafi is not in the Ayatollah Khomeini's league, still his reliance on and support for terrorism is well known and also needs to be challenged vigorously. We identified at least 25 terrorist incidents last year involving Libyan agents or surrogates. The main target of Libyan terrorism was anti-Qadhafi exiles in Western Europe and the Middle East. In April 1984 a gunman fired from the Libyan People's Bureau, killing a British policewoman and wounding eleven anti-Qadhafi demonstrators. This occurred after two bombings which injured at least 30 people in London and Manchester. Following the siege of the People's Bureau in London, British police found weapons in the building. This further documents Libya's practice of stocking weapons and explosives in its embassies—a clear violation of international diplomatic conventions. And, I must say, that these attacks in high-populated British cities have passed without significant response.

Some of the many factions of the Palestine Liberation Organization also practice terrorism. PLO influence has somewhat diminished today due primarily to its defeat in Lebanon in 1982 and heightened factionalism. Still, many of its splinter groups remain a serious threat to Israel and to Western governments. Syria controls or at least influences some of the more radical groups in the PLO that are believed to be behind recent terrorist attacks on moderate Palestinians and other Arabs, especially Jordanian officials.

For several years, various European left-wing terrorist groups have called for the establishment of an international united front against "Western imperialism" and particularly against its most powerful symbols—NATO and the American presence in Europe. Since the summer of 1984 at least three of these groups, the West German Red Army Faction, the French group Direct Action, and the Belgian Communist Combatant Cells, have apparently collaborated in a concerted terrorist offensive against NATO that reached a fever pitch of violence by early February 1985. The terrorists carried out a rash of assassinations, and bombing attacks on institutions associated with NATO and the United States, and Western interests like the Atlantic Institute, West European Union, and the European Space Agency.

That, in brief, is a quick overview of who the terrorists are and where their violence is directed.

I'd like to turn for a moment to the Soviet connection. It may seem shadowy to some, but it seems rather clear to me. For example, Iran and the Soviet Union are hardly allies, but they both share a fundamental hostility to the West. When Iran, Libya and the PLO provide arms and training to the Sandinistas in Central America, they are aiding Soviet and Cuban efforts to undermine our security as well as the security of friendly countries and governments of that area. The Soviets and their East European allies have provided intelligence, weapons, funds, and training for Middle Eastern terrorists at camps in the Soviet Union and elsewhere in Eastern Europe—East Germany, Bulgaria, and Czechoslovakia. Those passing through these training camps receive indoctrination in Marxism-Leninism which provides a rationale for terrorism and violence against civilian targets—all in the name of "wars of national liberation."

We have seen, however, only indirect evidence of East Bloc involvement in the murders and bombings now carried out by the West Europeans themselves. Publicly the Soviets' posture is that they "disapprove" of terrorism and that they consider terrorism to be "leftist adventurism" and simplistic ideology. At the same time, we don't see the Soviets taking any action whatsoever to assist victimized governments in curbing terrorist activities. The Soviet Union and its East European allies frequently permit West

European terrorists to transit their territory enroute to the Middle East. Moreover, some East European countries have been uncooperative in the extradition of terrorists on international arrest warrants. It is also interesting to note that relatively few Soviet and East European targets worldwide have been the victims of terrorist attacks.

The fact is, however, that we perceive the Soviets as having changed their operational techniques. In recent years they have become increasingly sophisticated in their use of active measures against the West. The Soviets now can achieve their aims quite well indirectly by providing training to selected individuals and very small groups, by providing logistic support to these groups, and upon occasion by providing weapons, explosives, and intelligence to the terrorist groups. They make little attempt to conceal the extent of their financial and military aid for countries like Libya and Syria—countries that have adopted terrorism as part of their state policy. The Soviets are quite willing to sell Libya any weapons it requires, and the Syrians also receive considerable quantities of arms from the Soviets. We know that many of these weapons are passed along to Palestinian groups for use in Lebanon and Israel. Some of these weapons eventually find their way to radical groups far from the hills of Lebanon.

Even more serious is the continuing willingness of Moscow and its allies to allow radical groups to maintain offices in Eastern Europe and to grant safe passage to operatives traveling to Western Europe or other destinations for the purpose of carrying out terrorist acts. No one can seriously believe that these activities, which have gone on for at least fifteen years, have escaped the notice of the Communist authorities.

The chain extends around the globe. Part of the subversive threat we face in Central America is stimulated by outsiders who are well-versed in terrorism. For example, Italian Prime Minister Craxi stated in early February that Nicaragua hosts 44 of Italy's most dangerous terrorists. This statement is corroborated in part by a former Red Brigade terrorist who said that at least six of his former comrades now serve as non-commissioned officers in the Sandinista army.

Nicaragua, by the way, is a major recipient of aid from Qadhafi's Libya and recently played host to Iranian Prime Minister Musavi. It is not surprising that the same names and faces keep turning up whenever we look broadly at the subject of international terrorism.

I'd like now to turn briefly to the rather murky area of collusion between the drug/narcotics people and the terrorists and their supporters. Drug dealers see their interests as being the corruption and gradual control or manipulation of the established regime to include the buying of policemen, security agents, judges, members of parliament, and even premiers. Money is the means and also the object for narcotics pushers. Terrorists, on the other hand, are out to destroy the existing system. If they had their way, they would not corrupt the policemen and judges—they would kill them. Moreover, money is useful for buying weapons, paying operational expenses, and buying intelligence and other information. But the terrorist is above all ideological, not mercenary. He is committed to overthrowing the established regime—that is his objective.

This said, there is a degree of cooperation between some terrorists and narcotics groups for at least tactical reasons. For example, a symbiotic relationship has grown up in Colombia between the narcotics dealers along the Caribbean coast and the revolutionary armed forces. Neither group ordinarily would have much to do with one another. But the drug merchant needs a secure transit point for his goods to reach markets in the United States. One such transit point is Cuba and the waters around Cuba. And the terrorists need arms.

In the past, the Cubans funneled arms and money to the guerrilla groups through drug merchant channels, so there is compatibility and complementary interest. Although when speaking with American journalists, Fidel Castro loudly denies having dealings with drug merchants, in fact we have caught him red-handed. By helping drug dealers push cocaine and marijuana, Castro gains improved access to the Cuban community in South Florida, contributes to crime and disorder in the United States, and aids his revolutionary offspring in Colombia.

Terrorist methods are becoming increasingly sophisticated. Explosives, remotely detonated or set off by a fanatical suicide-vehicle driver, are examples of both technical and tactical innovation. And all of the risks associated with terrorism are greatly diminished by the involvement of governments in the planning, financing, training, documentation, and providing of safehaven for terrorist groups. With the help of a sponsoring state, these groups are able to use more sophisticated techniques because of state-funded training programs, and more deadly, more difficult-to-detect equipment and arms. They also receive intelligence, and get official travel documents—sometimes used as diplomatic cover to hide their true identities. This support makes it easy for terrorists to mask movements and munitions deliveries—and then find safehaven in a sponsoring state after an attack. So the backing of governments enormously escalates the scope and the power of this growing threat.

Radical states—those I mentioned, maybe others—see in terrorism the potential for obtaining concessions from other states that can never be obtained by traditional diplomatic means. Our very ability to endure in our policies is being called into question by terrorism. Our decision-making process can be disrupted, confidence in the workability of our institutions can be eroded, and—unless we deal effectively with terrorism—our international credibility will be seriously weakened. This happened at the time of the Iranian hostage crisis some five years ago. Perhaps worst of all, terrorism has become a tempting instrument for some groups hoping to accelerate social, political, and economic collapse in target countries. In the final analysis, that is where the main thrust is likely to be.

In several European and Latin American states, small numbers of revolutionaries, disdainful of the electoral process and unable to win popular support through the ballot box, have succeeded in subverting the climate of opinion from one that respected parliamentary debate into one that encourages blows and counter-blows, violence and counter-violence. This has resulted in the gradual weakening of parliamentary institutions and democratic processes. Clearly, the Soviet Union and its allies have grasped the potential of terrorist movements for disrupting societies, particularly in the Third World. Clearly, they recognized that in Africa, Asia, and Latin America there are many weak governments with low levels of legitimacy and high levels of instability. To a degree far greater than is generally realized, these governments are acutely vulnerable to terrorist disruptions and are, therefore, tempting targets for terrorist campaigns.

In providing terrorist movements with arms, training, and political support, the Soviet Union and its allies, the radical states, have discovered a highly cost-effective way of making the point that in today's world, it is not safe to practice democracy.

Now let me talk for a few moments on another question. How do we cope with these small bands of highly-trained people? Most of them are fanatics, ready to give up life itself to do their evil work, and increasingly sophisticated as they move around the world crossing borders easily with official and professionally-prepared papers. As they travel, they know they will have no trouble getting weapons, explosives, and whatever else they need near the site of their intended attack. They know, too, that they will be able to find protection and sanctuary prearranged for them. We can combat this only with the highest professionalism, dedication, diligence, and commitment. We need to know and understand the various terrorist groups—their style and operating methods, their support structures, and their training camps which sprout up around the world. This is a task of continuing collection and analysis of intelligence in which the civilized nations of the world need to cooperate closely. We need to provide security and protection for our people and our facilities. We need to provide the most advanced security and police methods. But against a threat which can move so quickly, widely, and quietly none of us can do it alone.

With increasing tempo and effectiveness we are developing a worldwide counter-terrorist network. It is made up of the intelligence, security, and police organizations of certain nations. They exchange intelligence and share data banks. They work together operationally, provide training and technical capabilities to the less advanced of their number, undertake surveillance and other intelligence assignments for each other, report their findings, transmit alerts and warnings, and join in responding and defending against terrorist threats. That is really where it has to be done.

No one nation is going to be able to do it alone. It has to be done in a broadly collaborative way, with close day-to-day cooperation between the intelligence, security, and police services of nations around the world.

Now, terrorist groups are very tough nuts for intelligence to crack. That is almost self-evident. They are small, not easily penetrated, and their operations are closely held and compartmented. Only a few people in the organization are privy to specific operations, they move quickly, and place a very high premium on secrecy and surprise. Yet prompt reporting and follow-up action does frequently forestall terrorist incidents. The most common example is forewarning to U.S. and foreign embassies or other institutions of actual threats, or strong indications of planning for attacks on institutions and individuals. The usual response to this kind of knowledge is heightened alert, increased protective measures, or changes in plans and schedules which frequently disrupts the terrorists' plans and results in a failure or a decision not to make the attempt.

Recently, for example, intelligence on a threatened hijacking of a foreign commercial airliner, combined with effective police work, resulted in a change of travel plans which prevented the intended hijacking. In other instances, in Europe, the Middle East, Africa, and Latin America, U.S. officials and businessmen directly targeted by terrorists have been temporarily removed from their posts. On several occasions, warning and detailed intelligence has directly assisted foreign authorities in capturing terrorists and thwarting their evil programs. Sharing of intelligence on terrorist plans and the whereabouts of known or suspected terrorists is another way these services can assist each other. So this process of cooperation does work and is productive.

On the other hand, it does produce many false alarms. The volume of threat reporting has almost invariably escalated dramatically in the wake of a headline-making terrorist incident. At such a time, some individuals seek to market information that they know has become saleable. At the same time, our own intelligence collectors are energized by major terrorist events to ferret out any information—even seemingly marginal details—concerning possible planning for attacks that could threaten U.S. lives and property. The flip side of this is that when such threat reporting increases, more reports of dubious credibility tend to make it through the system that normally would filter them out. And this can also produce false confirmations. So it's a very delicate process of handling and sifting out these reports. We've made rather good progress, I believe, in developing a system for very rapid communication within and between governments to gather assessments, have reports tested by intelligence experts throughout our government and others, and pass conclusions and assessments along quickly to the point of threat.

Now, let me turn briefly to the question of policy. What is our policy in dealing with terrorism?

Well, the practice of international terrorism has to be resisted by all legal means. Perpetrators and sponsors of terrorist acts must be held accountable for their deeds. Whenever we obtain evidence that an act of terrorism is about to be mounted against our interests or our friends, we will take measures to warn and protect our citizens, property and interests, and our friends and allies as well. Terrorism is a common problem for all democratic nations, and we must work intensely with other countries to eliminate this threat to our free and open society. This is our fundamental long-term challenge and commitment. We will use every possible diplomatic and political avenue to persuade those now practicing and supporting terrorism, or who assist in acts of state-sponsored and organized terrorism, that they will be appropriately exposed and condemned in every available forum. That's the sort of broad perspective and attitude toward this phenomenon.

Our own government is now engaged in large-scale efforts to improve the physical security of our diplomatic missions and overseas facilities. Training programs are now mandatory for sensitizing our diplomatic and military personnel to the nature of the terrorist threat. And steps that every individual can take to improve personal protection from terrorist attack are being drilled into people. We are working closely with many other governments to improve the quality of security that is provided to our personnel abroad. We work with local governments to improve their capabilities whenever possible. And we are expanding our own capability to provide additional protection to foreign diplomats and dignitaries who visit us here in our own country. That is at the security and protective level.

Now on the response level, the United States does not use force indiscriminately. But we must be free to consider an armed strike against terrorists and those who support them, where elimination of the threat does not appear to be feasible by any other means. We face very difficult and sensitive problems in choosing appropriate instruments and responses in each case. Yet we cannot allow this to freeze us into paralysis. That's exactly what the terrorists now expect and would like to have happen. Just as we will not bargain—and that, as you know, has been for some years our declared policy—we will respond when circumstances are appropriate and we have the necessary information. We cannot and will not abstain from forcible action to prevent, preempt, or respond to terrorist acts where the conditions justify—indeed, our knowledge justifies—the use of force.

Many countries, including the United States, have the specific force and capability needed to carry out operations against terrorist groups. If that capability is not used when and where it is clearly justified, we lose both the direct benefits of action and the deterrent value of having the capability to retaliate. And we need that deterrent. We cannot permit terrorist groups or their sponsors to feel they can make free and unopposed use of violence against us. We must demonstrate our will to meet a terrorist's challenge with measured force, applied quickly, whenever the evidence warrants. We cannot permit terrorists and their sponsoring states to feel that we are inhibited from responding, or that our response is going to be so bogged down in interminable consultations or debates that we, in fact, do not really have a deterrent.

International terrorism is the ultimate abuse of human rights. We should be prepared to direct a proportional military response against bona fide military targets of those states which direct terrorist actions against us. And we need not insist on absolute evidence that the targets were used solely to support terrorism. Nor should we need to prove beyond all reasonable doubt that a particular element or individual in that state is responsible for specific terrorist acts. For example, there is sufficient evidence that radical Shia terrorists are responsive to Iranian guidance and receive Ira-

nian support on a constant basis, for us to hold Tehran responsible
for their attacks against United States citizens, properties, and interests.

Now, the legitimacy of using force against terrorism depends
on our willingness to make strong efforts to deal with this threat
by means short of force. Physical security, training, diplomatic efforts, the improvement of institutions for sharing our resources
and knowledge with other countries, the force of law, all these
measures must be applied in integrated fashion and they must be
applied as rigorously as possible. We must continue to improve
our ability to wield all the elements of national power—political,
economic, diplomatic, military, and informational—against the
scourge of terrorism.

In my view, Western nations have, on the whole, been weak
in applying economic, political, and diplomatic sanctions and
measures to check state terrorism. Sanctions, when exercised in
concert with other nations, can help to isolate, weaken, or punish
states that sponsor terrorism. Too often, countries are inhibited by
fear of losing commercial opportunities or fear of provoking further terrorism. It is true that economic sanctions and other forms
of countervailing pressure impose costs and risks on nations that
apply them, but some sacrifices will be necessary if we are not to
suffer even greater costs down the road. Examples of how the international community can move in concert are the 1973 Convention for the Suppression of Unlawful Acts Against the Safety of
Civil Aviation—a concerted measure taken to deal with the hijackings of the early 1970s, the Montreal Convention, and the
1979 International Convention Against the Taking of Hostages.
The international community needs to put teeth in existing agreements of this sort by severely punishing violations—and many nations have been slow on this.

And today there are still other initiatives that might be taken
bilaterally and multilaterally if we are to deal with terrorism effectively. For example, we should review international treaties
and agreements that define diplomatic privilege to identify standards of diplomatic practice and behavior which should be vigorously enforced. We may need new international measures to
counter misuse of diplomatic privileges by states sponsoring terrorist activities.

Although the issue of extradition is dealt with bilaterally under normal circumstances, terrorism violates all civilized norms. We should therefore think about developing multilateral treaties whereby persons who commit terrorist acts against citizens of any signatory state could be routinely extradited. Moreover, individuals who use false passports and other documentation and who have crossed international boundaries should be detained and an investigation begun to determine the purpose of their travel. Rules also should exist whereby individuals known to be involved in terrorism can be prevented from entering any signatory state. And there are other such measures that can be taken to tighten up on the investigation of terrorist organizations and protect against their evil activities. It would be an important signal to those nations that have signed existing counter-terrorism conventions and agreements if other nations which have not yet signed proceeded to ratify them swiftly. Five European nations, for example, have yet to ratify the Strasbourg Convention on the suppression of terrorism.

The reality—the bottom line—is that terrorism aims at the very heart of civilization. We have no realistic choice but to meet it, and that means head on. Nothing else will work. And the aim of the terrorists and the ultimate objective for those who sponsor, train, encourage and supply terrorists, is to undermine our values, to shatter our self-confidence, and to thwart our response. In the absence of a national will to fight terrorism at its roots, we must be content only to cope with terrorism's effects—not its cause. And that will not be enough.

But a strong beginning has been made. Parliaments have begun to authorize funds for combatting terrorism, and governments have begun to establish effective counter-terrorism units. Governments are increasingly working closely together, and intelligence and security services are developing new capabilities and improving their methods and performance.

A conference such as this goes far to air the very tough and difficult issues I've tried to outline for you this evening. In dealing with terrorism, strong public attention will be needed to focus meaningful action by our government and others in response to this threat. Thank you very much.

TERRORISM[3]

A Worldwide Trend[*]

It would be useful to define terrorism as a universally recognized crime. Old passions and new hatreds, however, make it difficult to find a definition of terrorism that would be universally acceptable.

In the distorted view of Moslem fundamentalists, the suicide bombers who destroyed the barracks of the U.S. and French peacekeeping forces in Lebanon, killing hundreds of soldiers, were heroes. In the view of the Irish Republican Army (IRA), the same is true of those who, on the pretext of supporting Northern Ireland's independence, massacre innocent civilians in London. Fanatic Basque irredentists, Italy's Red Brigades, and Peru's Sendero Luminoso have made assassination a form of political activism.

What does terrorism represent today, whatever its objectives and obvious manipulations? A UN debate organized to define terrorism did not go beyond theoretical discussions—the theory being that terrorism is a byproduct of misery, oppression, hunger, and other terrible situations in which communities, peoples, and nations find themselves. The proponents of this thesis have applied it to terrorism in the developing world—in places such as the Middle East, Asia, Latin America, and Africa.

But this theory, a blend of legalism and what passes for Marxism, loses its substance when confronted with the facts. To accept it would be to believe that the miserable conditions that supposedly engender terrorism are prevalent in Spain, Italy, Great Britain, and Germany. In all of these nations there has been terrorism as cruel as any in the Third World.

It is increasingly evident that terrorists of various nationalities and motivations are not simply autonomous agents struggling for diverse causes. There are links among their actions. The weapons,

[3]A selection of articles from the foreign press. *World Press Review.* 32:35+. S. '85. Reprinted by permission.

[*] This report by Frederico Branco is excerpted from the conservative *Jornal da Tarde* of São Paulo.

bombs, and other equipment used by IRA assassins, for example, are identical to those used by the Basque killers.

Certain airports are consistently attractive to terrorists: those airports denounced by the International Pilots Assn. Finally, the target of terrorism is always the same: the West and its institutions, beginning with the U.S. and the democratic nations of Western Europe and extending to their allies around the world.

Faced with this situation, it is less important to arrive at a definition of terrorism than to end its dissemination. Any vacillations—such as Greece's giving in to the TWA hijackers, Americans' subsidizing of IRA gunmen, or allowing security relaxation at the world's airports—serves to encourage terrorists.

No airport security measures can be 100 per cent effective. Terrorists always find ways around them. They know how to exploit human reluctance to employ rigorous security measures; they find sympathizers who will smuggle arms on board airplanes before takeoff; and they will find countries where their activities are not only tolerated but also praised.

Then how can we put an end to terrorism? Only by employing international action, perfectly coordinated and sustained by firm political will. Most Western nations appear ready and willing to cooperate.

Unfortunately, that is not true for the huge part of the world under the direct influence of the Soviet Union. The Soviet superpower has not hesitated to cooperate with terrorism. That was clear in its reactions to the bombings of the American and French compounds in Beirut and to the TWA hijacking. These attacks and kidnappings, according to Moscow, are simply a response to Western "complicity"—particularly by the United States—in Israel's Middle East policies.

Such an attitude constitutes the greatest incentive to terrorists. This problem has not escaped the attention of Western diplomats. It will have to be on the agenda of the meeting planned for November in Geneva between President Reagan and Soviet leader Mikhail Gorbachev.

The rising tide of terror can be contained only with the active cooperation of the Soviet Union. Perhaps this is a price that Gorbachev will be ready to pay in return for Western cooperation in helping the Soviet Union achieve economic recovery, an important goal for the new leader.

The first fully coordinated international action against terrorism may depend on what the superpowers decide in Geneva. That would still leave state terrorism unresolved. But that is another story, an even more complicated and sinister one.

Terror and Democracy[*]

The greatest proportion of terrorist operations—36 per cent of the world total—occur in Western Europe, according to statistics on terrorism in the early 1980s. The Middle East is second with 21 per cent, followed by Latin America with 19 per cent, North America with 9 per cent, Asia with 5 per cent, and Africa with 3 per cent. Terrorism in the U.S.S.R. and Eastern Europe accounts for only 3 per cent of the total, with the remainder distributed among other countries such as Australia and Oceania.

These figures suggest that about half of all terrorist operations occur in countries with democratic governments. Students of terrorism offer several reasons for the low incidence of terrorism in totalitarian countries.

The first reason is that most terrorist groups are leftist and therefore are not inclined to commit terrorist acts in Communist countries. Another reason is that totalitarian governments directly control the press and broadcast media in their countries and have an iron grip on the gathering and diffusion of news. These governments are in a position to suppress any information concerning terrorist acts committed against them. Finally, security provisions and police powers are unrestricted in Communist countries, making the apprehension of terrorists and the suppression of their activities relatively easy.

Should democratic governments violate democratic principles and individual freedoms in order to fight terrorism? This is an extremely important question, because if the answer is yes, these governments face a difficult choice. Either they must maintain the rule of uncompromising democracy and tolerate the evils of terrorism, or they must sacrifice some democratic freedoms to eliminate terrorism.

[*]This report by Amhed Jalal Izzeddin is excerpted from the semiofficial *Al-Ahram* of Cairo.

Citizens of today's democratic societies have voluntarily relinquished certain personal freedoms to protect themselves from terrorism. Airplane passengers, for example, permit searches of their persons and of their baggage. They know that this inconvenience may save them from hijackers who would commandeer their planes to unwanted destinations and hold them hostage for a cause they neither support nor understand.

This logic has prompted many democratic governments to take security measures against terrorism. Such provisions compromise constitutional freedoms, but then have been enacted without public protest because they protect national security and the cause of democracy.

It is significant that except for popular movements of national liberation and self-determination, most terrorist organizations represent intellectual or ideological minorities that can impose their beliefs on society at large only through terrorism, "the weapon of the weak." These groups pursue two goals vis-à-vis democratic government.

They want to demonstrate the weakness of a regime that is powerless to protect its citizens and institutions at home and abroad. They also want to force the regime to fight terrorism by adopting the repressive measures of a police state, legitimizing the terrorists' actions as just resistance to tyranny.

To protect national security and democracy, many democratic governments have enacted special laws to fight terrorism. Britain and West Germany, both known for their respect for freedom, have passed such laws.

In 1973 the British Parliament approved the Emergency Measures Law to deal with terrorist organizations in Northern Ireland. In 1974 the law was amended and a committee was appointed to study anti-terrorist measures and their effects on civilian and human rights. British law enforcement agencies were given wider powers of search, arrest, and detainment, and judicial procedures were changed to relax the rules of evidence in cases relating to terrorist crimes.

In the same year, after a terrorist attack in Birmingham killed twenty-one people, the House of Commons granted British police additional powers, including the right to deport those connected with terrorist activities in other countries and to hold citizens and aliens without trial for up to seven days.

West Germany enacted laws that widened governmental powers of search, arrest, and detainment so that, for example, suspects accused of terrorist crimes could be tried without legal counsel. German anti-terrorist laws are similar to their British counterparts, with one critical difference. The British provisions are temporary and come up for renewal at regular intervals, while Germany's are permanent.

Guilt and Innocence*

Terrorism has been the hallmark of the recent past, with a toll of three vacationers at Frankfurt airport, thirteen people at a café in San Salvador, seventy-five bystanders in Tripoli, 329 passengers and crew of an Air India jet off the coast of Ireland, and one man murdered in the Beirut hijack saga. The motives behind these acts of barbarism may have differed, but their consequences were identical. The victims had no connection with the causes the killers espoused.

Were the U.S. hostages in Beirut to blame for the Shiites imprisoned in Israel? What had the two children massacred at Frankfurt airport done to harm anyone? The bomb on the Air India airliner killed both Hindus and Sikhs, "oppressors" and "oppressed."

Dirty tricks respect no one; that, from the terrorists' point of view, is what makes them so effective. The aim is not to give some tyrant who is to blame for their predicament his just desserts. It is to fill the hearts and minds of everyone with fear and anxiety.

Terrorism remains effective, as classical reactions to the recent spate of massacres attest. Outrage and disgust give way to a feeling of helplessness. Only the victims are visible; the faceless killer vanishes either in the international underground or under cover provided by a cooperating government.

A quest for sense and punishment soon follows. As members of a social state governed by the rule of law, we begin to wonder what the "true" reasons for terrorism are. Accustomed to seeking

*This report by Josef Joffe is excerpted from the independent *Süddeutsche Zeitung* of Munich.

motives for more mundane crimes, we grow prepared to show "understanding" to the murderer with purportedly political motives.

The quest always follows the same pattern. When people lob grenades or plant bombs, we feel that it is terrible—but we believe that it might be a cry for help from people who are oppressed, desperate, and unable otherwise to gain a hearing.

Did the Israelis not breach international law in imprisoning 700 Shiites? Was this offense not the reason for the TWA hijacking? Besides, the Shiites have for decades been an oppressed community in Lebanon. Is it surprising for the underprivileged to run amok sooner or later? At first glance the logic of this argument seems striking. Yet it carries no weight because it merges guilt and innocence. We have almost absolved of blame what is inexcusable. Worse still, this argument brings us perilously close to the logic of the terrorists themselves.

Pragmatic understanding is not the way to deal with this moral arrogance. In the fanatic's distorted view, his suffering towers above all other. Whatever appalling misdeed he may commit, it is nothing compared with what he or his comrades have suffered.

"Even if you have to blow up half a continent and shed a sea of blood to destroy the part of barbarity," German revolutionary Karl Heinzen (1809–80) wrote, "have no qualms about doing so." Of what consequence are the lives of a handful of people when the future of the world is at stake?

We may feel political sympathy with one group or another and sound out the root causes of violence, but we must never fall into the moral trap the terrorist sets. The injustice cannot be offset by understanding—and by fresh injustice. Nor is terrorism a stroke of fate that must be borne patiently like an earthquake or a flood.

Terrorism subsists on the vulnerability of a Western world unwilling to resort to totalitarian methods. Between 1968 and 1980, 6,700 acts of terrorism were registered around the world, but they included only sixty-two in the Eastern Bloc. Yet a free society can push the price of terror sky-high without jeopardizing its freedom, as Germany did in fighting the Red Army Faction in 1977.

Terrorism need not be understood; it must be prevented and, failing that, avenged if the culprits can be identified. Understanding, even though it may be deeply rooted in the Western sense of justice, will not tame the beast. It will merely encourage it.

'Born' in the U.S.*

Now that the Syrian Pharaoh has let Ronald Reagan's people go, it surely would be churlish to belittle their bondage in Lebanon. After all, one of the TWA passengers was callously murdered early on, and the remaining captives underwent scarcely more reassuring trials under the klieg lights. Anyone with a claim to decency must have sympathized and wished them well.

That said, however, a qualifying postscript seems due. Though the thirty-nine Americans were not hostage for anything near their Teheran-held compatriots' 444 days, there were times when it seemed that long. U.S. journalists have a natural interest in their own people, but so lavish and obsessive was the coverage that almost all other news was drowned out for the period.

It was "the most dramatic international crisis" since the Iran hostages were freed five years ago, one New York publication ruled. And all this after the Air India jetliner—probably a target of terrorism as well—plunged into the North Atlantic Ocean with 329 victims.

Robert McFarlane, President Reagan's national security adviser, mused that punishment ought to "focus our power on dealing with the root causes of terrorism—where people are trained, where they are housed, fed, sustained." A leading newspaper furiously noted how much of that training, "intent on eliminating Western values," takes place in the Soviet bloc, Libya, Cuba, and North Korea. What no commentator remarked on was that Sikh terrorists accused of plotting Rajiv Gandhi's murder, and suspected of having sabotaged the Air India jet, had been trained and sustained in the state of Alabama.

If 329 Americans had been bombed into the ocean, as most investigators believe the Air India travelers were, questions about Frank Camper's Reconnaissance Commando School would be fly-

*This report is excerpted from the newsmagazine *Asiaweek* of Hong Kong.

ing thicker than ceasefires in Lebanon. As it is, there are all sorts of questions that are begging to be asked.

The Sikhs charged with conspiring to kill Gandhi took a $350, two-week course at Camper's guerrilla-warfare center last November, learning about timebombs, silent killing, and other edifying fare. They attended this school near Birmingham after they had approached an undercover FBI agent. According to FBI reports, the agent continually cited this arms base while dealing with the Sikhs from January to May 3, when they acquired a gun in Birmingham to kill an Indian official in New Orleans.

Four suspects were arrested in New Orleans on May 4, but between then and May 13, when the arrests were announced, Lal Singh and Ammand Singh, two alleged accomplices, simply disappeared. Both are now suspects in the Air India crash and the Tokyo airport explosion.

Mr. Camper professes shock that Lal Singh might have been a terrorist, though the Sikhs reportedly talked about blowing up bridges and nuclear power plants. "I would have done anything in my power to stop him," says Camper. But the Sikhs, who were enrolled with no questions asked, were not at the school to study needlepoint.

Though U.S. authorities say that the "school" violates no apparent law, this seems to carry academic freedom to absurdity. Most graduates, it appears, are would-be Rambos eager to chew up the jungle against Nicaragua's Sandinista government.

To that end, perhaps, Washington has turned a blind eye. Unquestionably, members of the political hit-man profession have drawn most aid behind the Iron Curtain. But if McFarlane wants to know where freelance terrorists can learn their trade he need look no further than Dixie.

FLAKE OR FOX?[4]

I find he's not only a barbarian, but he's flaky.

Ronald Reagan said it with a smile, savoring his own use of the vernacular. When a reporter asked whether Reagan seriously meant to describe Libyan leader Muammar Kaddafi as mentally unbalanced, the president explained affably that "flaky" was merely a "term we use in conversation with someone." He was calling Kaddafi "a zealot" and a threat to peace—but not, evidently, a madman. When last week's news conference ended, the president was still chuckling over his choice of words. A bit smugly, he asked his aides: "How would 'flaky' translate in Arabic?"

But Reagan had other, harsher words for Kaddafi, and he spoke them completely in earnest. He accused Libya of committing "armed aggression against the United States" by supporting the Palestinian terrorists who butchered 15 travelers, including five Americans, at the Rome and Vienna airports on Dec. 27. In retaliation, the president imposed a trade embargo on Libya, ordered all Americans working there to leave the country and froze the Libyan government's financial assets in the United States. Those steps were likely to cause only limited trouble for Kaddafi, largely because Washington's allies were generally unwilling to go along with economic sanctions. "There's no point beating the air with a sword," said French Prime Minister Laurent Fabius, predicting that sanctions would be "ineffective." To Europe's relief, Reagan had concluded, for the time being, that military action against Libya would be even more counterproductive. He chose the cautious course, but his secretary of state warned that Washington's patience was running out. "Force is not always the best means," said George Shultz, "but it may be necessary on occasion."

[4]Reprint of an article by Russell Watson, John Walcott, Kim Willenson, and Zofia Smardz, wi*
Newsweek bureau reporters. *Newsweek*. 107:14–20. Ja. 20, '86. Copyright © 1986 by Newsweek, Inc
rights reserved. Reprinted with permission.

Junk mail: Some outraged Americans thought the time already had come to punish Kaddafi for sponsoring international terrorism. Democratic Sen. Howard Metzenbaum of Ohio told a television interviewer that "maybe we're at that point in the world where Mr. Kaddafi has to be eliminated." In a survey by polltaker Louis Harris, large majorities endorsed punitive action against meddlers like Libya; 72 percent of the people surveyed said that countries supporting terrorism should be threatened with invasion, while 79 percent advocated a universal death penalty for terrorists. A more pungent form of protest came from fed-up Americans who tried to mail their household garbage to Kaddafi (a gesture not encouraged by the Postal Service). The gathering public outcry left the Reagan administration exactly where it wanted to be. "We're a half step behind the newspapers and the congressmen," exulted one policymaker. "They're asking why we aren't acting, not why we are."

In fact, Washington was prepared to do a lot more, despite the fact that the evidence linking Kaddafi to the particular atrocities in Rome and Vienna was circumstantial at best. The administration drafted a far-reaching plan to tighten the economic and political screws on Kaddafi, to fuel dissent inside his country, to contain Libyan-sponsored terrorism and to clear the way for a military attack on Libya if Kaddafi is foolish enough to provide the United States with another good excuse. One senior official said the plan "will increase the pressure on Kaddafi, make it harder for him to strike back . . . and maybe even get rid of him entirely."

Suicide squads: One thing was certain: Kaddafi won't go quietly. The attention he received from Reagan provoked the Libyan leader into a new outburst of reckless rhetoric. At a news conference in Tripoli, his capital, he called the president a "stinking, rotten crusader" and "an aging, third-rate actor." Later he invited Reagan to visit him in his tent, so that the president could see for
[don't live in trenches with hand grenades in my
i charged that the American embargo was
olitically to a declaration of war" and warned that
iing "suicide groups" to respond to any U.S. attack.
n us at home, we shall threaten them at home," he
afi praised Sabri al Banna, better known as Abu

Nidal, the Palestinian terrorist leader blamed for the Christmas killings. "If Abu Nidal is a terrorist," he said, "then so is George Washington." And he warned that if American hostility continued, his Islamic nation just might turn communist.

Kaddafi's tirades did sound a bit flaky. But how unstable is he? For that matter, how strong is the evidence connecting him to terror and subversion around the world? And how does a ruler of fewer than 4 million people get away with being the world's most conspicuous troublemaker?

How His Mind Works

Egypt's Anwar Sadat once claimed that Kaddafi was "100 percent sick and possessed of the demon." Another old foe, former Sudanese President Jaafar Nimeiry, diagnosed him as "a split personality—both evil." Even his admirers concede that Kaddafi is moody, hot tempered and unpredictable. An administration official argues that Kaddafi "displays behavior typical of many sociopaths or psychopaths—extremely warm one moment, then hostile and cold the next." Unproven but persistent rumors speak of secret treatments in a Swiss sanitarium years ago. But there is no solid clinical evidence on which to base a judgment about Kaddafi's mental health, which forces analysts to rely on their own instincts. Former CIA Director Richard Helms, who has extensive experience in the Middle East, concludes that "Kaddafi is in some respects crazy like a fox. His various moves, even though seemingly outlandish, appear to have some strategic or tactical motive behind them. I think he's peculiar, quixotic, eccentric. But I don't think he's crazy by any means."

In large part, Kaddafi is a product of Bedouin culture. He was born 43 years ago, the son of a shepherd who lived in a goatskin tent in northern Libya, a region steeped in poverty despite the oil that enriched a few under the Libyan monarchy. Kaddafi took to the gospel of revolution at an early age, modeling himself at various times on Egypt's Gamal Abdel Nasser and China's Mao Tsetung, among others. He learned a little English at a school in Tripoli and studied briefly in England, where he felt like an outsider, he says now. Back in Libya, he joined the Army, married a former nurse and eventually fathered seven children. In 1969 Kaddafi and a small group of fellow officers overthrew King Idris and steered Libya on to a radically new course.

Reflecting his nomadic tribal background, Kaddafi instinctively opposes the rich and powerful and resists any form of political structure and the impediments that go with it. Under his leadership, Libya has been transformed into *al Jamahiriyah*—"the state of the masses." The oil wealth has been widely redistributed. Kaddafi's political, social and economic ideas, some of them distinctly half-baked, are spelled out in the three slim volumes of his Green Book, self-consciously modeled on Mao's Little Red Book. "No representation in lieu of the people" is its overriding principle— the idea that everyone should share in government, town-meeting style. In practice, however, the Green Book concedes that any society will be ruled by the strong—in this case, Kaddafi. The colonel holds no formal job in the state; he is simply *al Qaid*, The Leader.

"Kaddafi's foremost ambition is to dominate and unite the Arab world," says a white paper released by the State Department last week. "He frequently compares himself to Garibaldi or Bismarck and has justified his use of violence and terrorism against moderate Arab regimes as necessary to achieve Arab unity." Kaddafi is also an egotist and a crybaby who sulks or throws tantrums when he doesn't get what he wants. He can act prudently and will even back down when he has to. But a study by the CIA and other U.S. intelligence agencies predicted a year ago that Kaddafi will never change. "We concluded that there is a zero probability that Kaddafi will abandon his dream of uniting the Arab world under his leadership and of humiliating the United States," says an administration official, "and an equally remote chance that he will abandon terrorism as his principal weapon."

The Case against Him

Surveying the evidence that links Kaddafi to the killings in Rome and Vienna, Robert Oakley, the head of the State Department's counterterrorism office, conceded last week: "We have no smoking pistol." In fact, the only tangible evidence that investigators in Europe had come up with so far were two Tunisian passports, confiscated from guest workers in Libya and eventually supplied to two of the Palestinian gunmen as part of their cover. According to Austrian Interior Minister Karl Blecha, there was no proof of direct Libyan involvement in the terrorist operation. The two gunmen who survived the Vienna attack "said they had not been in Libya and had not been trained there," Blecha told reporters. In fact, there were signs that the gunmen may have been trained in Syrian-controlled Lebanon and traveled to Europe by way of Damascus.

Syria has a history of supporting Abu Nidal, but the last thing the administration wanted to find out was that Syrian President Hafez Assad might have to share some of the blame for the attacks. Washington is trying to encourage Assad to play a peacemaking role in the Middle East and to help negotiate the release of the remaining American hostages in Lebanon. "Syria is continuing to support Abu Nidal," Oakley conceded last week, but "not at the same level as before, which I think is a blessing for all concerned. We hope that they will stop." If Syria doesn't back off, he said, sanctions might be imposed on Damascus.

Kaddafi denies any responsibility for the incidents in Rome and Vienna, and last week he urged Palestinian "freedom fighters" to limit themselves to "military Israeli targets." Oakley insisted, however, that there was another strong link between Abu Nidal and Libya. "Since early 1984, Libya began to provide increased support to the group and Abu Nidal himself, and many of the group's operations may have been moved there within the last 12 months," he said. Oakley discerned "a pattern of activity" suggesting that Abu Nidal was now serving Libyan interests, as well as his own. The group's bloody hijacking of an Egyptian airliner last November struck a blow at one of Kaddafi's major enemies. "It all falls into place," said Oakley. "It doesn't leave any doubt in my mind as to what we're dealing with."

Abu Nidal is only one of Kaddafi's protégés, according to the administration. "He is harboring terrorists," said Shultz. "He is providing them financial support. He is providing them a certain kind of infrastructure. He is involved. He is a terrorist." The State Department white paper charges that Kaddafi "operates numerous training camps for foreign dissident groups." Then why doesn't the administration provide photographs or at least descriptions of the camps? "If we published satellite photographs," said Oakley, they would have shown nothing but "a group of tents. We would have said, 'There are terrorists in those tents.' Kaddafi would have said, 'They're Boy Scouts.' There would have been a huge debate in the media. It would have made the situation more difficult rather than easier."

Smoking pistols: The case against Kaddafi may be only circumstantial where the Rome and Vienna attacks are concerned, but elsewhere there are smoking pistols aplenty. An assassination campaign targeted against Libyan dissidents living abroad accounts for 31 of the 58 specific terrorist incidents cited in the white paper. Libyan exiles have been gunned down and bombed all over Europe, and innocent bystanders have been caught in the cross fire, including the British policewoman who was shot to death outside the Libyan Embassy in London in 1984. One of Kaddafi's hit squads tried to kill a former Libyan prime minister in Egypt 14 months ago. That attempt was a disastrous flop; the plotters were arrested and Kaddafi was tricked into announcing that the victim had been killed. He also has tried to kill opponents in the United States. A Libyan exile in Colorado was wounded by a hired assassin in 1981, and last May a Libyan diplomat at the United Nations was expelled in connection with an alleged plot against the lives of Libyan dissidents in four states.

Kaddafi also is known for political subversion in the Arab world and for military intervention in sub-Saharan Africa. At one time or another, he has managed to stir up trouble with Egypt, Sudan, Tunisia and Algeria. He sent troops to Uganda to support the bloodthirsty Idi Amin. And since 1973 he has been waging an off-again-on-again war for control of Chad, the mineral-rich country to the south. In 1984 Kaddafi double-crossed the French, who had withdrawn their troops from Chad, by leaving his own forces in control of the northern part of the country. According to the State Department white paper, Libya "views black Africa as a principal arena for forging a group of anti-Western radical states that will strengthen Libyan influence . . . and confer upon Kaddafi status as a world leader."

So far, he is mainly a leader of terrorists—or at least their most adventurous patron. Over the years Kaddafi has helped the Irish Republican Army, the Basque and Corsican separatists, the Moro guerrillas in the Philippines and leftists in Central America. In 1984 and 1985, according to the State Department, armed Libyan "pilgrims" tried to disrupt the annual hajj to Muslim holy places in Saudi Arabia. Four years ago Washington claimed that Kaddafi had sent hit teams to the United States to murder President Reagan and other leaders. And last May, again according to the State Department, "the Egyptians thwarted a plot by radical Palestinians backed by Libya to destroy the U.S. Embassy in Cairo with a truck bomb." Kaddafi is not the only sponsor of international terrorism. "The problem won't go away if he does," says former administration analyst Dennis Ross, "but it won't get any better as long as he's around."

How He Gets Away With It

Kaddafi's oil wealth helps to explain why he gets away with so much troublemaking. Last week he called in West European ambassadors and courted them with carrot and stick. Kaddafi warned that if the United States attacked Libya, "we will drag Europe into it." But he also alluded to the economic benefits that Europe could reap by staying on his good side—the job openings created by departing Americans, the contracts that soon would be up for grabs. "The Europeans don't have the political will or the backbone to do what needs to be done to cope with terrorism," charged Yonah Alexander, a terrorism expert at Georgetown University. "The short-term benefits are more important to them than their long-term interests."

Yet the West Europeans already were fighting a war against terrorism on their own soil, a conflict that hasn't really spread to the United States so far. They have taken tough security measures, and some of them, notably the French, have sharply reduced their trade with Libya. But many European leaders, including such staunch allies as Margaret Thatcher and Helmut Kohl, maintain that economic sanctions don't work—the same position that Ronald Reagan took on the 1980 U.S. grain embargo that seemed to do more harm to American farmers than to the Soviet invaders of Afghanistan.

Kaddafi gets a little additional protection from his relationship with the Soviet Union. He is far too quirky to be an ideal Soviet client, but he gives the Kremlin a political beachhead in the Middle East, and he pays top petrodollar for Soviet military equipment—more of it, in fact, than his scrawny armed forces can use. In Moscow last October, Kaddafi pulled off a diplomatic coup by wangling three meetings with the Soviet leader Mikhail Gorbachev, who now seems willing to support Libya's territorial claim in the Gulf of Sidra. Last week the Soviets expressed support for Libya and accused Washington of "gunboat diplomacy." American officials don't think Moscow would go to the mat to save Kaddafi, economically or militarily. But they note that the Kremlin has supplied Libya with SAM-5 antiaircraft missiles, and they believe that Gorbachev is determined to maintain a high profile in the Third World.

Arab solidarity: The American embargo and the implicit threat of military action forced even moderate Arabs to rally behind Kaddafi. Saudi Arabia and Sudan, targets of Kaddafi schemes in the past, issued statements of support. So did Egypt, which had sent troops toward the Libyan border after the airline hijacking in November; now the Egyptians have moved the Fourth Armored Division, their best striking force, away from the frontier. The 45-member Islamic Conference organization passed a resolution of solidarity with Libya. "President Reagan's orders and measures will not hurt Kaddafi," said M. T. Mehdi, president of the American-Arab Relations Committee. "Rather, they will increase his popularity from Jakarta to Casablanca."

Kaddafi's hold on the affections of his own people may not be so secure. Because of the current world oil glut, Libya's petroleum income has dropped sharply, forcing a cut in imports and a decline in the standard of living. A Western diplomat in Tripoli estimates that "the discontent level has reached 95 percent." Most outsiders assume that change can come only through an upheaval by the armed forces. Kaddafi has always looked after his Army, but lately he has allowed Libya's revolutionary committees—politically powerful groups similar to the Revolutionary Guards in Iran—to replace some high-ranking officers, and more assaults on the brass are expected. As a result, there are rumors of unsuccessful attempts on Kaddafi's life, and recently one of his cousins, an influential colonel, was assassinated. Libya itself could turn out to be Kaddafi's weak spot. If he falls, it may not be because of his support for terrorism or his other dirty dealings overseas, but because he got careless at home.

III. MISMANAGING TERRORISM

EDITOR'S INTRODUCTION

The election of Ronald Reagan in 1980 was due in part to his promise to deal sternly with terrorism. The Iranian hostage crisis of 1979–80 had made President Carter look weak and ineffectual—never more so than when an abortive attempt to rescue the hostages ended with the death of eight American servicemen. The so-called Shultz Doctrine, articulated by Reagan's secretary of state, George Shultz, in October 1984, holds that our response to international terrorism "should go beyond passive defense to consider means of active prevention, preemption, and retaliation."

But this rhetoric has not been supported by action. Although far more American lives were taken by terrorists during the first five years of the Reagan Administration than under any previous administration, only one act of reprisal—the capture by U.S. warplanes of the Egyptian jet carrying the *Achille Lauro* hijackers—has been at all successful. To its embarrassment, the United States has found that it often cannot positively identify or locate the perpetrators, that it does not have the intelligence apparatus to infiltrate most terrorist groups, and that it cannot (or will not, for strategic reasons) impose effective sanctions against the states that support them. Critics of the administration claim that the rise in terrorism against Americans can in part be traced to the disparity between American words and actions; empty threats only breed contempt among the terrorists, who know that they can strike with impunity.

There is also confusion within the Reagan Administration about which kinds of terrorists it should attack and which it should support. While denouncing international terrorism, the administration has been pressing Congress for money to support the internal "antiterrorist programs" of some oppressive regimes—programs that may include as their targets members of legitimate opposition parties and human rights groups. In the first selection, Daniel Treisman, in a report for *The New Republic*, points out the contradictions of administration policies on antiterrorism as they apply to Central America.

Our poor record in antiterrorism, at least outside the United States, is partly the fault of the news media, especially television news. The networks, in their search for marketable programming, have played up stories of hijacking and other attacks in sensational fashion. They have been singularly helpful in publicizing terrorists' demands and providing a stage for their bloody performances. The second selection, from *Harper's* magazine, is a round-table discussion by prominent newsmen and writers of the relationship between the media and terrorism. The third and fourth articles, reprinted from *Commentary* and *American Spectator*, analyze the most notorious of recent "collaborations" between television and the terrorists, the staged interviews with the hostages of TWA Flight 847.

TERROR ERROR[1]

What exactly is terrorism? Administration officials such as Secretary of State George Shultz view it as a malignant strain of geopolitical AIDS, eroding the immune system of the international body politic, inducing confusion and paralysis. In the State Department's official definition, it is "the threat or use of violence for political purposes by individuals or groups whether acting for or in opposition to established governmental authority when such actions are intended to shock, stun, or intimidate a target group wider than the immediate victims." Whatever else, terrorism is violence against innocent noncombatants. Elaborating on such definitions has become one of the thriving cottage industries of academe.

In late July 1984 the elite, U.S.-trained Atlacatl Battalion of the El Salvador army swept through the village of Los Llanitos

[1]Reprint of an article by reporter Daniel Treisman. *The New Republic*. 193:16+. O. 14, '85. Copyright © 1985 by *The New Republic*. All rights reserved. Reprinted by permission.

in the northern mountains of El Salvador. The soldiers smashed the roofs of houses, cut down corn, and then spread out through the surrounding countryside to track down the villagers who had fled. Antonio Lobo was hiding in a ravine with his family and others. "The army descended by the river and got to about five meters from us," he told Tutela Legal, the human rights agency of the Salvadoran Catholic Church. "They did not give us any warning and just shot at us." About 80 civilians were killed in similar incidents around Los Llanitos during the next few days.

In a bizarre development, those who initiated the Los Llanitos massacre may soon receive U.S. funding—in the name of fighting terrorism. A State Department memorandum recently leaked to *The Washington Post* outlines a plan to provide $27 million in military support and $26 million in police training funds to El Salvador, Guatemala, Honduras, Costa Rica, and Panama. The money will go to buy everything from X-ray equipment to Bell 212 helicopters and M-16 rifles. Drafted shortly after the June 19 terrorist attack on a San Salvador café that left four Marines dead, the proposal reflects the administration's determination to fight the "terrorist threat" worldwide. And, by the logic of the State Department, this requires shipping weapons to the raiders of Los Llanitos (and their counterparts in Guatemala). What matters to the administration is less the nature of the terrorist act than the political views of its perpetrators.

The U.S. has been training other countries' security forces in antiterrorist operations for 18 months under the Anti-Terrorism Assistance Program. But the State Department's new proposal allocates for Central America alone over five times the 1985 budget for antiterrorist training worldwide. And as well as seminars, the new program would provide arms and advanced security equipment. The $22 million earmarked for El Salvador will presumably add to the $483 million in economic and military assistance already requested by the administration and authorized in the foreign aid bill. Because of Guatemala's history of army brutality, the administration has been unable to persuade Congress to authorize more than the most meager military aid to that country. Counterterrorism is a politically irresistible pretext to reopen the flow of arms.

Aid to Guatemala, the memo says, is needed to "reiterate our support of that government's decision to go forward with elections" this November. Yet the Guatemalan government has made no request for U.S. military aid this year and, according to the Guatemalan Embassy in Washington, does not intend to. The army's heavy hand is already felt guiding the election process, endorsing a candidate, and defining the narrow limits of debate. Last March Guatemala's head of state, General Humberto Mejia Victores, declared that the country's only human rights agency, the Mutual Support Group for the Families of the Disappeared, was infiltrated by "subversives." Just a few days later, four armed men kidnapped one of the group's leaders, beat him to death, and cut out his tongue. Another of the group's leaders was found murdered at the bottom of a ravine along with her three-year-old son and younger brother. Overwhelming evidence exists that the army has indiscriminately murdered Indian peasants in rural areas. No member of the armed forces has ever been detained, much less tried or convicted, for such offenses.

In these circumstances, more military aid will hardly strengthen the hand of those committed to the democratic process and a return to civilian rule. And there's little sign that Guatemala's military leaders intend to change their ways. General Mejia Victores persistently denies any army involvement in human rights abuses. Guatemala should not be singled out for criticism, he told a press conference last July. "It seems there is also terrorism in the whole world."

In El Salvador incidents such as the Los Llanitos massacre are the outgrowth of official policy. In order to deny guerrilla forces food and support, peasants in certain areas are driven from their homes with grenades and rifles. In Chalatenango province, Colonel Sigifredo Ochoa has established 12 "free-fire" zones. "In these zones there are no civilians," Colonel Ochoa told Chris Hedges of *The Dallas Morning News.* "There are only concentrations of guerrillas, so we keep these areas under heavy fire." In fact, according to relief officials Hedges interviewed, these areas *are* populated by civilians.

The Guatemalan government's indiscriminate attacks against unarmed Indian peasants also constitute terror. And an admirably succinct definition of terrorism—"Selective Use of Violence for Propagandistic Effects"—appears as a chapter heading in the manual drafted by the CIA for the Nicaraguan *contras'* instruction. If it were serious about its own definition, the State Department would have to include Nicaragua among the recipients of counterterrorism aid. Clearly the administration's position is not entirely ingenuous.

Whatever they may say, administration officials do not consider each act of terror around the world an equal offense to the American way of life. Only those judged to threaten U.S. interests meet with a firm response. The real danger, according to President Reagan, is "terrorism that is part of a pattern, the work of a confederation of terrorist states" whose "goal is to expel America from the world." And in Central America the focal point of this anti-American alliance, in Reagan's view, is Nicaragua.

For a government to ignore its country's geopolitical interests would be a dereliction of duty. But the strategic perspective can be misleadingly seductive. One danger to El Salvador's democracy, according to the State Department's memo, is "leftist-instigated labor and student unrest." In fact, union discontent frequently originates in labor groups that supported Salvadoran president José Napoleón Duarte. For the most part, their demands are neither revolutionary nor antidemocratic, and they pose no threat to U.S. interests. Besides pressing for wage increases to keep up with the cost of living, most want Duarte to fulfill his campaign promises to prosecute political assassins and continue the dialogue with the guerrillas.

The foolishness of responding to labor protest with counterterrorist SWAT teams was amply demonstrated in June. A special unit of the Salvadoran treasury police, trained by the U.S., stormed a hospital in San Salvador to break a month-long strike. Shortly before dawn, over 100 troops occupied the building, streaming in through the basement and from a helicopter on the roof. Patients and medical staff were forced to lie down with their hands tied behind their backs. In the confusion four undercover police officers were killed by the troops.

The counterterrorism proposal is particularly disquieting in view of certain attitudes in the State Department. In recent years senior officials have tried to discredit human rights reporting groups who don't share the administration's selective definition of terrorism. On ABC's "Nightline" last February, former secretary of state for human rights Elliott Abrams flatly denied that the Los Llanitos massacre ever happened: "I'm telling you that there were no significant—there were no massacres in El Salvador in 1984." Not only did *The New York Times*, *The Boston Globe*, and *The Miami Herald* confirm that the massacre took place, even the Salvadoran government's own Human Rights Commission admitted that 80 civilians were killed there "out of combat." State Department officials who investigated the case say that, although there were casualties at Los Llanitos, there was no evidence to indicate a massacre and much evidence to indicate that the guerrillas stage-managed the incident.

Abrams's denials were part of a larger campaign to discredit anyone who suggests that U.S.-backed military forces in the region have committed abuses that qualify as terrorism. In September 1982 Assistant Secretary of State for Inter-American Affairs Thomas Enders (whose job Abrams now holds) circulated a letter attacking an Amnesty International report on human rights violations in Guatemala. Embassy information, Enders declared, "frequently contrasts sharply with that provided by Amnesty International." This was something of an overstatement: in three of the seven cases Enders cited there was no significant difference between the embassy's and Amnesty's accounts. In the other four cases Amnesty relied on a more stringent standard of evidence than the embassy.

Enders, who allowed the letter to be distributed to the Guatemalan press, had worked on Central American policy long enough to know that such public criticism might be taken by the military as permission to attack the offending organization. Enders's actions, according to a report by the Americas Watch Committee, "contributed to circumstances in which, if Amnesty wished to send a mission to that country, the mission's members—and its sources—would not be safe."

Similarly, the administration has also attempted to discredit Tutela Legal by disputing its connection to the Salvadoran Catholic Church. This puts it strangely at odds with Archbishop Arturo Rivera y Damas, who has issued a statement calling Tutela Legal an "important and close part" of his ministry.

To base Central American policy on strategic interests of the U.S. as well as human rights is only reasonable. But the question of strategy should not be smuggled through Congress behind a screen of metal detectors. By packaging military aid as counterterrorism, the administration hopes to deliver aid Congress might otherwise be reluctant to send. Few members of Congress are naive enough to be taken in by this semantic chicanery. But most can read the political signs. Any measure termed "antiterrorism" is bound to draw a flurry of supportive constituent letters. The bill, which will emerge later this fall, is considered likely to pass with only minor "damage limitation" amendments. "It'll really fly," laments one congressional aide.

TERRORISM AND THE MEDIA: A DISCUSSION[2]

TED KOPPEL, moderator of this discussion, is anchorman of the ABC News programs *Nightline* and *Viewpoint*.

NORMAN PODHORETZ is the editor of *Commentary*.

CHARLES KRAUTHAMMER is a senior editor of the *New Republic* and a contributing essayist at *Time*.

ALAIN BESANCON is a professor of the history of Russian culture at the École des Hautes Études in Paris and a columnist for *L'Express*.

JOHN O'SULLIVAN is an assistant editor and columnist at the London *Daily Telegraph*.

DANIEL SCHORR is senior correspondent of Cable News Network.

[2]Excerpted from the proceedings of a conference on international terrorism at the Jonathan Institute, June 1983. Reprinted from the Oct. 1984 issue of *Harper's*. All rights reserved. Reprinted with special permission.

GEORGE WILL is a columnist whose articles appear regularly in newspapers across the country.

BOB WOODWARD is an assistant managing editor of the *Washington Post*.

Ted Koppel: Let me put forward the proposition that the media, particularly television, and terrorists need one another, that they have what is fundamentally a symbiotic relationship. Without television, terrorism becomes rather like the philosopher's hypothetical tree falling in the forest: no one hears it fall and therefore it has no reason for being. And television without terrorism, while not deprived of all interesting things in the world, is nonetheless deprived of one of the most interesting.

Norman Podhoretz: Certainly terrorists and the media have had a symbiotic relationship, which has helped give the lie to those pious proclamations on the editorial pages that organizations like the PLO, by engaging in terrorism, hurt their own cause. On the contrary, it is clear that, for a long time, because of this symbiotic relationship, the power and influence of such organizations increased with each new terrorist act.

In the last few years, however, this relationship has been disrupted by what I call Robert Nisbet's law, which states that boredom is the most underrated force in human affairs. After the 10,000th hijacking or wanton assassination, the media have become bored, and their coverage has accordingly declined. Much less attention is paid to terrorist episodes these days than even five years ago. Insofar as this prevents terrorist organizations from achieving their principal objective, which is to get a lot of publicity, this development is good news. But it also indicates how accustomed the public has grown to these acts: we are no longer as horrified by them as we should be. Terrorist outrages are now taken for granted, as are the subtle exculpations that the media help propagate; for example, that terrorism represents a protest against intolerable social conditions or that it is a form of guerrilla warfare. Such exculpations have so taken hold that they now govern the public's response to terrorism.

Charles Krauthammer: I think Mr. Podhoretz is right in saying that a kind of boredom is setting in. Airplane hijackings, for example, are now covered on the inside pages of most newspapers. But terrorists are rather resourceful about creating new theatrical productions; every year or two they come up with a new variant that captures the media's imagination. The most recent innovation is the suicide bombing, such as the attack on the American marines in Lebanon and on the U.S. Embassy in Kuwait.

But we should remember that not all terrorism is dependent on the media. When we discuss terrorism we are really talking about at least three different kinds of political violence. The first and oldest kind is assassination, the usual form of political violence before World War II. The political assassin does not need the media to explain what his act means; in fact, often he does not want publicity at all. His object is simply to eliminate a political actor.

The second form of terrorism, which emerged after the war, is the random attack on civilians, but civilians of a particular type—civilians who are members of the enemy class or nationality. Terrorism of this sort, as practiced, for example, by the FLN in Algeria in the late 1950s and early 1960s, is also independent of the media. Its object is to demoralize the enemy during a war, and its audience is the victim himself and his compatriots. In the case of Algeria, it was the *pieds noirs*, the French living there.

The third and newest form of terrorism, which the PLO largely created after 1968, is the random attack on anyone. We might refer to this as "media terrorism," for it can exist only if there is an interpreter to give it meaning. The terrorist acts of the PLO were not intended to demoralize the Israelis—the PLO has never really been at war with Israel—but to publicize political grievances. And the intended audience was not the immediate victims—the airline passengers—or even the Israelis, but the entire world. For such actions, coverage by the mass media becomes absolutely essential. This is where terrorists' utter dependence on the media begins.

Media terrorism—such as the 1975 murder of three Dutchmen who happened to be on a commuter train hijacked by Moluccans, or the 1976 seizure of Yugoslavian hostages by Croatian terrorists—is a form of political advertising. In the latter instance, the Croatians demanded that U.S. newspapers publish their manifesto. Since the outlaws cannot buy television time, they have to earn it through terrorist acts. Like the sponsors of early television who produced shows as vehicles for their commercials, media terrorists now provide drama—murder and kidnapping, live—in return for advertising time.

The media's responsibility to act with self-restraint is obviously greatest with this kind of terrorism. In those cases where the victim is chosen at random and has no connection whatever with any political struggle, terrorism is actually a lure to attract the media. Through his acts, the terrorist tries to earn a stage on which to proclaim his message. And the media then take upon themselves the duty of interpreting those acts. In 1979, for example, terrorists attacked the American Embassy in Beirut with grenades. One network correspondent explained that this action was "perhaps an expression of resentment and frustration" on the part of Palestinians over the Israeli-Egyptian peace treaty. Here we reach a level where an attack on innocents is rationalized as a psychological necessity. Or consider the attack on a bus near Tel Aviv last April: it was generally explained as the PLO's assertion that it still existed after its expulsion from Lebanon, a kind of "I kill, therefore I am." Without the press to carry this message, the act would have been meaningless; in fact, since it had no military or political purpose, it probably would not have been committed in the first place. I believe that when the point of a terrorist attack is to force the media to function as interpreters, the media have a heavy responsibility not to do the interpreting.

Koppel: You mentioned Algeria. Perhaps Mr. Besançon could tell us whether there was censorship in France with regard to the terrorism in Algeria. To what degree was the French press manipulated by the government or by the terrorist groups?

Alain Besançon: There was no real censorship in France during the war in Algeria, in spite of the widespread terrorism there. With a few exceptions, those who favored Algerian independence expressed themselves freely. I was a young man at the beginning of the war, serving in the French army. I favored independence for Algeria, but mainly to protect the democratic structure of France. For what ultimately made terrorism possible during the war—and the situation was similar for England during the conflict in Ireland in the 1920s—what made terrorism possible was the democratic system of the parent nations. England had to choose between remaining democratic or holding on to Ireland. France had to choose between remaining democratic or holding on to Algeria.

Koppel: Mr. O'Sullivan, would you comment on the conflict that arises when a democracy confronts terrorism: Does one oppose terrorism by using methods that are nondemocratic—such as censoring the press—or by so doing does one undermine democracy itself?

John O'Sullivan: If we consider the terrorism in Northern Ireland for a moment, quite plainly certain prohibitions apply that are not part and parcel of the normal rule of law. For example, although there are no serious restrictions on the press or television in Britain, there is a very important restriction on television in the Irish Republic. This directive, issued, by the way, by Conor Cruise O'Brien when he was minister of posts and telegraphs, forbids the broadcasting of interviews with IRA members. Why is this? Because, as Dr. O'Brien said, "We in the Irish state regard the appearance of terrorists on television as an incitement to murder." The incitement is addressed not so much to the general public as to other terrorists and potential terrorists. Such appearances glamorize these people. Since they have little support among the population, they could not give their views on television and be treated respectfully if they had not engaged in a campaign of murder.

Television is a leveling and homogenizing medium. It is very difficult to interview terrorists without presenting them not as a species of criminal but as a species of politician. You may try to interview a terrorist toughly, to ask searching questions and make plain that he is a murderer, and yet it is difficult to imagine how anyone could be grilled more toughly than, say, Dan Rather grilled Mr. Nixon.

I myself am perfectly prepared to support a ban on interviews with terrorists in Northern Ireland, since the only justification advanced for such interviews—namely, that we need to know what the terrorists' views are—is absurd. We know what their views are before they ever appear on television.

Koppel: Dan Schorr, can such limits on the media be legitimately imposed in a democracy?

Daniel Schorr: Let me say first, Ted, that it's entirely appropriate that you preside over this discussion, since you are one of
the few Americans, along with Ronald Reagan, whose career has
benefited from terrorist activities. I'm referring, of course, to
ABC's extensive coverage of the seizure of the American hostages
in Iran in 1979.

What Charles Krauthammer said is true: there was terrorism
before there was television. Lincoln was assassinated in the Ford
Theater, the archduke was assassinated in Sarajevo, and television
wasn't there, although I am sure it would like to have been. But
in our society television and violence have a mutual attraction that
is very, very dangerous. Television has become the arbiter of who
is important, who has identity. Many people have found that the
royal road to identity is to do something violent. Television has
a love affair with drama and a love affair with violence. We must
find some way to keep this love affair under control. Consider
what happened here in Washington in 1977 when the Hanafi
Muslims seized the B'nai B'rith building and held 134 people hostage. Now that was certainly a great story. But was it necessary
to have round-the-clock coverage by all the local television stations? The leader of the Hanafi Muslims, holed up in the B'nai
B'rith building with his hostages, spent his time watching himself
on television. At one point he called his wife to ask, "How am I
doing?"

Media terrorism is primarily a television problem. Being on
television confers a kind of reality on people, much more so than
being written about in the newspaper. But what should TV journalists do? Not cover terrorist events? Well, obviously not—we
are in the news business. But we don't have to provide live coverage when nothing is really happening. We don't have to telephone
terrorists and ask them to give live interviews. I suggest that we
in the news business impose some voluntary limits, because if we
don't, there may come a time when they are imposed on us.

George Will: To think that the press holds the key to the
problem of terrorism is not uncustomary narcissism on the part
of the journalistic profession. What can we really do to diminish
the incentive for publicity? I suggest it's precious little. If terrorists
take over an embassy in the center of London or seize an American

ambassador or shoot a pope, people are going to notice. It doesn't matter whether you have a policy about how many hours you're on the air. Terrorists will achieve their magnifying effect, which is what they use the media for. And in a country that is blessed—or, depending on your point of view, afflicted—with a First Amendment, it is quite impossible, given how the law has recently been construed, to enforce any kind of prior restraint. Absent enforcement from a fourth party, the competition between the three major networks virtually guarantees that there will be maximum coverage of anything spectacular and telegenic.

Perhaps one problem lies in our definition of the term "terrorist." I don't think we ought to say that John Wilkes Booth or Gavrilo Princip were terrorists, although certainly they had political aims. The dominant kind of terrorism today, the kind we should be discussing, is what Secretary of State Shultz has called state-sponsored terrorism. Such terrorism is used by certain states as an instrument of rational policy; it is not a television psychodrama, and thus is far beyond the capacity of journalists to deal with. And it is only the beginning of clarity to understand that just as revolutions are made not by bad water or bad schools or hungry people but by revolutionaries, so terrorism is made not by television but by terrorists. Terrorists make terrorism for the same reason people make potato chips—it pays. When it doesn't pay, they'll quit making potato chips and they'll quit making terrorism. And I think it would be a mistake to assume that the public is apt to grow bored very soon. The "Indiana Jones phenomenon" will undoubtedly come to affect terrorism—that is, just when the senses of the public seem saturated, terrorists will find new ways to lacerate people's sensibilities.

Bob Woodward: First of all, I don't think we are talking only about television, as Daniel Schorr said. We have to ask ourselves what sort of terrorism is politically most significant. I agree with George Will that it is the state-supported variety, and I think television is largely irrelevant to that. Consider the assassination of President-elect Bashir Gemayel in Lebanon in 1982. American intelligence agencies have established that the assassination was carried out by Syrian intelligence officers, and a credible case can be made that President Assad of Syria ordered it. Now this was a very alarming event. It changed the history and the politics of Lebanon. You don't need television to convey its importance, and the same can be said about the bombing of the marines in Beirut. The importance of the bombing was its military effect, not the fact that it was spectacular TV. I think the journalist's role in covering such events, whether he is a television reporter or a newspaper reporter, remains the traditional one—finding out who is responsible for them and then broadcasting or printing that information.

Besançon: Perhaps our real problem here is not so much defining terrorism as understanding the effect that terrorism publicized by the media can have on society. After all, most terrorism is undertaken in order to arouse the sympathy of society. So the question involves not simply journalism but the basic philosophical assumptions that are shared by the leaders of the cultural establishment. The ideology of most terrorist groups holds that capitalist society is doomed and does not deserve to be defended, that from its destruction something more worthwhile will emerge. This was the philosophy of the first large-scale terrorist movement, that of the Russian populists in the 1880s. Even Tolstoy, who espoused nonviolence, admired the ideas behind this movement. Or consider Jean-Paul Sartre. During his long life, Sartre advocated the terrorism of the Baader-Meinhof gang in Germany, the terrorism of the Red Brigades in Italy—he believed that there was a continuity between the eschatological hope of the terrorist and the reasonable need we all recognize to correct the flaws that exist in our society. I think this kind of sublime morality is very widespread and very difficult to eradicate. It is beyond the ability of the media to do so. This belief is most common among the highly educated, and it is from this group that most journalists and the leaders of the so-called cultural establishment are drawn.

O'Sullivan: This panel is composed of journalists from what is called the quality press. I suggest that the reporting on terrorism in the so-called popular press is much more accurate than it is in the more serious newspapers. Let's consider how each would describe an IRA bombing attack.

Popular newspapers like the *New York Post* or the *Daily Mail* in England would say: "A shy 21-year-old girl, whose only interest in life is tennis, was last night fighting for her life in a London hospital after being blown up in a restaurant by an IRA bomb. By her bedside was her fiancé, Gordon Williamson, 23. 'She didn't have an enemy in the world,' he said."

The *New York Times* or the *Guardian* would report something quite different: "Two people were killed and one injured in an IRA explosion in London last night. Government sources interpreted the explosion as a response to the government's decision to introduce a bill increasing parliamentary representation for Ulster. Sources in Belfast believed to be close to the IRA said that the attack was the start of a major campaign in which targets on the British mainland would not be exempt."

The assumption of the popular press is that terrorists are important for what they *do*. The assumption of the quality press is that terrorists are important for what they *say*. I suggest that the first assumption is much more sensible.

Alan Chalfont:[*] Perhaps the real problem with the media, or at least with the quality press, is its tendency to adopt a position of magisterial objectivity between our society and those attacking it. Norman Podhoretz said that the media subtly excuse certain terrorist acts by implying that they arise out of intolerable social conditions or intolerable oppression. We see these justifications as well in the media's tendency to equate the actions of legitimate governments, such as that in El Salvador, in fighting terrorists and revolutionaries with the activities of the terrorists themselves. Can we not simply accept the fact that we are at war with international terrorism, that there are two sides, ours and theirs? If their side prevails, our freedoms will disappear, and the first freedom to go will be freedom of the press. Is it too much to ask that, in a free society at war with international terrorism, the press should be on our side?

Krauthammer: Yes, it is too much to ask, unless the press takes the position that terrorism—defined as the indiscriminate attack on innocents to achieve political ends—is absolutely indefensible, a moral corruption begins that is irreversible. If we compromise that principle, then our profession that we stand for certain values is hollow, because high among those values is the

[*] Lord Chalfont, a former minister in the British Foreign Office, writes widely on international affairs.

belief that civilians ought to be exempt from attack. If there are people on our side who engage in the murder of civilians—for example, the gangsters who practice terrorism in El Salvador—they have to be condemned with as much vigor as those who do it in the name of another ideology.

Nonetheless it is true that the media have to change their rules when dealing with terrorism, because the terrorist act is of a different empirical reality than other events. In physics, the Heisenberg principle says that events are changed by being observed. The media have an obligation to apply their own Heisenberg principle. Journalists must recognize that there exists a unique class of political events, media terrorism; these acts acquire importance by, and often are undertaken with the sole intention of, being broadcast over the media. Because of the symbiotic relationship between the media and terrorist acts, because these acts are created or at least greatly amplified by media coverage, journalists must exercise self-restraint—call it censorship if you like. The rule of thumb I propose is this: In covering terrorist events, reporters ought to concentrate on who, what, where, and when. They should leave the question of why to the historians and the psychiatrists.

Woodward: I don't think any journalist would want to eliminate the "whys" from any story.

Schorr: We've been talking as if the problem is undue interference by the media, whereas the problem is really how terrorists manipulate the media. People who feel that the newspapers they read and the television news they watch should reflect their own personal views are making a very grave mistake. If we adopt this line of thinking, we will eventually have the kind of press that exists in Paris—a partisan press, in which everyone can find his own views reflected in his newspaper.

What is the responsibility of the press in covering terrorism? If a representative of a terrorist group approaches the *Washington Post* and says, "I want to try to explain to you who we are and what we are," Bob Woodward can write a gripping story describing who the terrorists are and what they believe. By writing this story he does not prevent the police from taking action against them. But if the government then forces him to betray the confidence that made the story possible, while a few people may be arrested, he will never get that kind of story again. Some of us still believe that journalists are people committed to the idea that the world must *know*. We believe that our job is to explain who terrorists are—whether they are right-wing terrorists or left-wing terrorists—without accepting the view of any one side. The free press can be destroyed very easily if it is polarized in the way that some have suggested here. We should examine the press in countries where it tries to satisfy the prejudices of particular groups—in France, the Soviet Union, Syria—before we start making new rules for ourselves.

Will: I agree with Charles Krauthammer that we should apply a sort of Heisenberg principle to the media. We in the media do effectively observe, but what we tend to observe, more often than events themselves, is the observers. We have heard today that the press has a double standard in covering terrorism. I think the alarming news is that there is a single standard, a wrong standard. You cannot underestimate the degree to which both sides, liberal and conservative, have a common view of the world that they simply cannot bear to have challenged. The view involves denial of the undeniable—the fact that we are under assault from the Soviet Union. That is how I read Claire Sterling's book on international terrorism, *The Terror Network*. Very few people, of whatever political persuasion, are willing to accept the reality of international terrorism. Our whole political culture has an enormous intellectual and psychological and emotional investment in a view of the world that international terrorism challenges. The media did not create this view; they merely serve to reflect the larger culture in which it is embedded.

Podhoretz: It has been said that the media should change the rules. I submit that the rules have already been changed. Some years back, the attitudes of the popular press that John O'Sullivan described were prevalent in the quality press as well. There was a time when our political culture was in fact a partisan of our side, when the journalist's role as a citizen did not conflict with his professional role. But in the later years of the Vietnam War this began to change. The passionate speeches we hear about objectivity and freedom of the press ring rather hollow today, because there is very little objectivity in the reporting of terrorist acts. Very often the terms that are used to characterize terrorists reveal a mindless bias—when Yasir Arafat is referred to as a moderate, for example. The media have become the most prominent exponents of these attitudes in the larger political culture, and I think this accounts for the widespread resentment of the press and TV. Many, many people, including myself, feel that the media are unsympathetic to our side in the struggle against totalitarianism and totalitarian communism.

Krauthammer: I find George Will uncharacteristically modest as to the importance and influence of the media. There can be no question that the development of enormously powerful communications technology, and the fact that this technology is in the hands of people who believe in competing with one another to get a good story, have produced a new phenomenon. The American hostages would not have been held so long had the Iranians not realized that they had created the most effective television stage in history, which gave them immediate access to millions of people. The Iranians exploited the hostage crisis in a way that they could not have done in the absence of television cameras.

Now, I want to give an example of the sort of media self-restraint that I am suggesting. In the late 1970s, there was a rash of episodes in which spectators at sporting events jumped out onto the playing field for their fifteen seconds of exposure on national television. After a number of these episodes, some of the networks decided to turn the cameras away. Instead, a reporter would say, "There's someone running out onto the field, but we won't show him to you because if we do, it will encourage other clowns to do the same thing." Now, when you hear the crowd cheering as the clowns are being chased off the field, you really want to see what is happening. But clearly it is worth forgoing that pleasure in order to gain a greater societal good—the nondisruption of future ball games. I think media executives should exercise the same self-restraint in covering terrorism, when the societal good to be gained is reducing the incentive to political murder.

Koppel: There is a great need to be aware of the proper roles in our society of journalists as well as of political leaders. When our leaders don't play the roles they should be playing, then the media is put in a totally irrational position. After all, it is not the job of the media to censor itself. Vietnam was mentioned a few minutes ago. Press censorship was never imposed during the Vietnam War because President Johnson was unwilling to pay the political price of a declaration of war. If indeed our leaders believe that we are in a state of war, then let it be declared. Once war is declared, then all kinds of societal pressures, and indeed legal pressures, come to bear on the media to play a different role than the one it plays right now.

But I urge you not to be in too much of a hurry to change the role that we in the media play, because once it has been changed, even for reasons that now seem valid, it may be difficult to change it back when the reasons are no longer so valid.

ISRAEL, THE HOSTAGES, AND THE NETWORKS[3]

The deterioration in U.S.-Israel relations in the year following the June 1982 invasion of Lebanon was among the steepest ever. It reached its nadir when a U.S. Marine waving a pistol at an Israeli tank was commended for "heroism" by the Pentagon, as if he had repulsed the armor of a hostile army.

Such attitudes in high places did not come out of nowhere. The extent to which television coverage conduced to them, for example, came to light in December 1984, when a prominent Senator confessed to a Jewish group that the reason he had recommended sanctions against Israel in 1982 was that television had convinced him Israel was perpetrating a holocaust in Lebanon.

But toward the end of 1983 the mood seemed to change. The bloody, hopelessly unresolvable sectarian conflicts in areas of Lebanon evacuated by Israel, the bombing of the American embassy and Marine barracks by suicidal Shiite fanatics, the Lebanese abrogation (under Syrian pressure) of the American-sponsored agreement with Israel, and the refusal of Syria to honor its pledge

[3]Reprint of an article by David Bar-Illan, a founding member of Artists & Writers for Peace in the Middle East. Commentary. 80:33+. S. '85. Copyright © 1985 by The American Jewish Committee. All rights reserved. Reprinted by permission.

to withdraw from Lebanon—all these Arab enormities served to create a more benevolent attitude toward Israel in Washington.

Not, however, in the media, and especially not among television reporters in the field. Whenever gorier than usual massacres occurred, reporters would surround the survivors to cajole, solicit, or prod anti-Israel statements from them. There was an almost symbiotic reciprocity in the transaction: the traumatized, homeless, and bereft, peering into the camera, would blame Israel's 1982 invasion for all the evil in Lebanon (a far safer exercise than blaming a rival sect), and the journalists for their part would discreetly refrain from questions about the twelve years of atrocities and bloodbaths which had preceded the invasion.

A particularly inflammatory flurry of media activity occurred just before Israel's final withdrawal. In response to sniping, car-bombing, and suicide attacks by the Shiite militias seeking credit for "forcing" Israel out of Lebanon, Israel implemented a "strong-hand" policy. The measures included the arrest of men caught carrying weapons and the blowing-up of houses in which arms caches had been found. These proved highly effective; but in a replay of their coverage of the 1982 invasion, the media depicted Israel's actions as indiscriminate attacks on civilians (none of the guerrillas wore uniforms), and they mistranslated the name of the operation as "iron fist," presumably in order to convey the idea of a brutal, ruthless repression.

Then came the accusation that two Lebanese cameramen serving as CBS stringers had been deliberately murdered by an Israeli tank crew. This was later retracted, without apology, when it became obvious that the Israeli troops had mistaken the cameramen for combatants. But the hyperbolic tone of the accusation, the rush to judgment on threadbare evidence, the repetition of a patently preposterous story, and the ill-concealed rage of virtually the entire industry were symptomatic. Characteristically, only one major newspaper in the whole country—the Boston *Globe* —published a photograph provided by the wire services showing that even from a distance of ten feet it was difficult to discern the difference between a TV camera and a shoulder-held anti-tank weapon used by the guerrillas. As was later proved, the Israeli tank was 1,000 yards away.

After Israel's withdrawal from the area south of Beirut, the Shiite Amal militia, in an attempt to establish hegemony over the area, attacked the Palestinian "camps" (really suburbs) of Sabra and Shatila. Children were shot dead point blank; men and women were dragged out of hospital beds and ambulances and killed; the sick and injured were left to die in the streets while Red Cross convoys were kept out of the area; huddling families in shelters were slaughtered in their sleep. Hundreds died, thousands were maimed and injured. But in the media these atrocities were underplayed and understated, in striking contrast to the coverage of the 1982 massacre in the same "camps," when Christian Arabs allied with Israel killed 450 men of military age and 35 women and children. The latter had probably received more air time and more inches of print in the American media than all the atrocities and massacres throughout the world since World War II combined.

Still, it was difficult to sustain the notion that this time the blame could be laid at Israel's doorstep. As the host of one of the talk shows put it, there was a growing feeling that the Arabs in Lebanon were "into killing."

All this changed overnight with the hijacking of TWA Flight 847. From the very beginning, the networks pounced on *one* of the hijackers' demands—the release of over 700 Lebanese detainees in Israel—to the exclusion of all of the others. Ignored was the demand for the release of 17 Shiite prisoners held in Kuwait, even though Kuwait's refusal to release them the preceding December had caused the murder of two American passengers by Shiite terrorists on a Kuwaiti plane hijacked to Teheran. Ignored was the fact that the release of these Shiite prisoners in Kuwait was also the stated purpose of kidnapping seven Americans in Beirut over the preceding sixteen months. Ignored, indeed, was the fact that this was the only demand which made sense, since the detainees in Israel were in the process of being released anyway.

Ignored, too, were the hijackers' other demands: the release of their cohort held by Greece; the release of two Shiite terrorists held by Spain; the reversal of America's policies in the Middle East; the ending of aid to Israel; and the overthrow of President Mubarak of Egypt and King Hussein of Jordan. When Israel's

Ambassador to the UN, on the ABC *Evening News*, pointed to these demands as a clear indication of the theatrical nature and propagandistic purposes of the hijacking, anchorman Peter Jennings cut him short and demanded to know if Israel would release the Shiite prisoners to save the hostages. Clearly, the only "viable" demand, so far as the media were concerned, was the release of the detainees.

The hijackers and their supporters, whose sensitivity to media techniques and moods has been a source of wonder to communication experts, were quick to recognize a public-relations bonanza when they saw it. By sticking to this one demand alone, they had television networks throughout the West acting as their mouthpiece, and at their disposal the 'round-the-clock services of the world's most influential opinion-molders. Like the media, they themselves quickly dropped all their other demands and concentrated on Israel.

So the familiar scene was set: on one side persecuted Arabs, "understandably enraged" by horrible injustices, making "reasonable" demands—after all, they were entitled to the release of those prisoners, said American arbitration experts paraded before the cameras—and on the other side intransigent Israelis coldbloodedly disregarding the fate of innocent people. (Israel, acting on the assumption that the President of the United States rather than the terrorists or their media mouthpieces represented American wishes, had taken its cue from official pronouncements and announced that it would not release the detainees under terrorist threats.)

Over and over again, television commentators, anchormen, and reporters, alternating hints with accusations, and assuming the roles of negotiators, arbiters, and moralizers, portrayed Israel as an ungrateful ally which had freed 1,150 convicted murderers in return for three Israeli soldiers, but would not free over 700 innocent Lebanese ("not charged with any crime") to save the lives of 39 American tourists. Thus, Bryant Gumbel of NBC's *Today* show, in a June 27 interview with Georgetown University Fellow Geoffrey Kemp, asked, "Will Israel compromise on the TWA hostages, or play fast and loose with American lives?" and "Is Israeli international politics going to take precedence over the well-being of the hostages?"

To buttress this campaign, a "split" was invented between the American and Israeli governments. On June 17, three days after the hijacking, the CBS *Evening News* reported a "diplomatic standoff" between the two countries. On the same evening, NBC reported that the U.S. was "frustrated" with Israel and that Secretary of State George P. Shultz was "annoyed." On June 21, CBS asserted that "Israel is trying to ease tensions with Washington," and ABC's *Nightline* reported that Israel was trying to smooth over "ruffled feathers." On July 1, Ted Koppel on *Nightline* wondered aloud if the U.S. "will begin to move away from Israel as a result of the hostage crisis."

All this time, such Israeli officials as Prime Minister Shimon Peres, Defense Minister Itzhak Rabin, Cabinet Minister Moshe Arens, Ambassador to the UN Benjamin Netanyahu, and Member of Parliament Ehud Olmert were flatly denying any differences between the two countries on the subject of the hostages. Nevertheless the networks persisted, oblivious to the fact that by pressuring Israel to release the Shiites they were also asking it to contravene the publicly and privately stated wishes of the American President, the Secretary of State, and the National Security Adviser.

Ironically, journalists who for years had criticized Israel for refusing to talk with the PLO suddenly discovered that Israel's long negotiations with a PLO faction, which had produced the exchange of 1,150 terrorists for three Israeli soldiers, were the root of all subsequent acts of terrorism not only in Lebanon but throughout the world. Blithely disregarding the endemic nature of terrorism in the Middle East, the anti-American thrust of world terrorism, and the eight hijackings in the months preceding the TWA incident—all perpetrated by Shiites and none connected to the detainees in Israel—Robert Novak, the syndicated columnist, averred on *Crossfire* on the Cable News Network (CNN) that the killing of six Americans in El Salvador, the blowing-up of the Air India flight over the Atlantic, and the explosions at the Frankfurt and Tokyo airports had all been triggered by Israel's release of the 1,150 PLO terrorists.

Throughout the seventeen-day ordeal, hardly a mention was made by TV newsmen of another possible explanation: that, as William Safire put it in his New York *Times* column, America's "fist-shaking warnings and tiptoeing backdowns after embassy bombings and the massacre of the Marines" might have encouraged terrorists to believe that they could hijack an American plane with impunity. On the contrary, when journalists were not blaming Israel for the hijacking, they were parroting the Shiite line that retribution for the murdered Marines had been exacted when the American battleship *New Jersey* shelled "Shiite villages," and that the "indiscriminate slaughter" caused by the shelling had in turn created bitter anti-American feelings which begat the hijacking. Yet as every newsman should have known, the *New Jersey* shelling had in fact been directed not at the Shiites but at the Druse militia and its allies advancing on the presidential palace in East Beirut and threatening to overthrow the legitimate government of Lebanon.

This was not the only Shiite interpretation of events adopted by newsmen. Shiite spokesmen contended that the TWA plane had been hijacked by men desperate to free "their relatives" held hostage in Israel, thus creating a parallel with the families of the American hostages who wanted the freedom of *their* relatives. Allyn Conwell, the hostages' spokesman, said: "If my wife and children were abducted and taken illegally across the border, I guess I, too, would have resorted to anything at all to free them."

Not a single reporter in Lebanon questioned these absurd statements, although surely even the most ignorant among them knew that there were no "wives and children" in Israeli custody but only young men of military age, all caught in actions against Israeli troops during the last phases of withdrawal from Lebanon. Even the inference, often made on television, that they had been taken as "insurance" against further attacks, was absurd. Had the Israelis wanted such "insurance," they would have arrested village elders, religious leaders, and sheiks. But except for Ted Koppel and George Will on ABC, and perhaps one or two others, no one protested this spurious parallel.

It should come as no surprise that the scenario of hostages on one side of the border and hostages on the other, conjuring a moral symmetry between the Arab hijackers and the Israeli army, proved irresistible. It was, after all, a pattern similar to that invoked by the media in speaking of the United States and the Soviet Union, both of whom are often portrayed as committing parallel crimes in comparable pursuits of hegemony. The Soviets invaded Afghanistan; we invaded Grenada. They shot down KAL Flight 007; we support atrocities by the *contras* in Nicaragua, etc. In line with such false and pernicious symmetries was the use of the word hostage, typically applied to kidnapped innocents whose lives are threatened, to describe detainees who were neither innocent nor threatened.

Similarly, much was made by the media of the "illegality" of Israel's holding of the prisoners, and its equivalence to the "illegality" of the hijacking. Both were said to be "violations of international law." Whether or not transferring the detainees to Israel actually constituted, as the U.S. State Department maintained, a violation of the Fourth Geneva Convention—and leading experts in international law adamantly insist it did not—to compare this kind of infraction (if such it was) to the TWA hijacking was like comparing a traffic violation to murder. None of the media analysts bothered to make the distinction. Nor did anyone seem to note that the Israeli rescue of hostages at Entebbe, the international pursuit of Mengele, and virtually all the proposed retaliatory measures against the hijackers (blockading the Beirut airport, apprehending the hijackers and bringing them to justice in America) were and are, strictly speaking, violations of international law.

During the entire crisis, the networks faithfully adhered to another bit of Shiite fiction: that the only "bad guys" were the first two hijackers who killed Navy diver Robert Stethem, that the dozen reinforcements who took over on the second Beirut stop were much more moderate and civilized, and that the Amal militiamen who removed the hostages from the plane and guarded them until their release were kind, gentle, and considerate saviors. It was one thing to hear such naive nonsense from the hostages, who, after witnessing a murder and expecting to be murdered themselves, would naturally consider anyone who did not kill them a savior;

it was another thing to hear it from presumably impartial and free agents.

For here again the facts were not secret: the reinforcements, who were invited to the plane by the original two, knew those two by name, gave them orders upon boarding, and worked in smooth collaboration with them through the next trip to Algiers and back to Beirut. Together they stripped the passengers of all their valuables; together they randomly beat them; and together they ordered the "selection" of those with Jewish-sounding names. The militiamen who transferred the hostages to "safe houses" in Beirut also acted with the full cooperation of the original hijackers. There was no altercation, not a harsh word, not the slightest disagreement. During the hostages' incarceration, the original hijackers, including the owner of the silver pistol who killed Stethem, were very much in evidence among the "good" militiamen, some of whom amused themselves by playing Russian roulette on the hostages. Finally, after the release, the two original hijackers appeared hooded at a press conference under Amal auspices.

Yet almost no one, in either the print or the electronic media, seemed to recognize this pattern, so similar to that followed in the Teheran hostage crisis of 1979. A lonely exception was the novelist, Mark Helprin, in the *Wall Street Journal* of July 1:

As in Iran, we have seen in the latest hostage drama the game of "hard cop/soft cop," in which the U.S. is put off balance by the alleged differences between a set of good guys and a set of bad guys. In Iran it was Bani-Sadr and Ghotbzadeh as opposed to Khomeini and the "students." In Lebanon, it was Messrs. Berri and Assad as opposed to the "hijackers" and the Hezbollah. Both crimes were adjuncts to local power struggles, but if what was true in Iran was true also in Lebanon, only one set of actors was in control, and the other was merely being used. In this context, it is interesting that the hijackers of TWA 847, supposedly uncompromising Islamic militants from whom Mr. Berri and Mr. Assad were to protect us, are reported to have consumed all the liquor on the plane and badly mistreated the women. Islamic militants certainly have their faults, but they rather studiously avoid such things. If the reports are true, who hijacked the plane in the first place? The operation was a lot more secular and political than some might think and was probably planned not in a mosque but in a ministry.

A few of the hostages were astute enough to recognize what the journalists ignored. Peter Hill insisted, after the release, that all the various groups had been in cahoots and there was no difference between them. For this, hostage-spokesman Allyn Conwell called him emotionally unstable and a racist. Hill and the other real heroes of the saga—the hostages who had refused to play talking puppets in the terrorist theater and who had presented a sullen and defiant visage to their captors' cameras—were practically ignored by the media after the release. Conwell, by contrast, became an overnight superstar, holding nationally televised press conferences, interviewed on national news programs, appearing alone on hour-long talk shows, and even endorsing Jimmy Carter's book on the Middle East, *The Blood of Abraham*. As the media critic Tom Shales observed (in the Washington *Post*, July 1): "The TV networks afforded Conwell the totally undeserved status of foreign-relations expert. When network anchors weren't playing diplomat themselves, they were putting Conwell on the air to play diplomat from his own wildly distorted vantage point."

The networks justified the numerous interviews with Conwell, before and after the release, by insisting that the American public had a right to know the viewpoint of the hostages' spokesman. They did not, however, insist on the viewers' right to know that Conwell ostentatiously carried Muslim prayer beads and the Koran throughout his captivity, and that he was a ten-year resident of an Arab country, Oman, where he represented an American company and to which he intended to return. Interestingly, when asked about his background, Conwell sometimes referred to "working overseas" in the last ten years, without mentioning Oman.

In portraying Amal chief Nabih Berri, the media again accepted the Shiite script, depicting him as a moderate negotiator, an impartial go-between trying his best to save both the Arab "hostages" in Israel and the American hostages in Beirut. What the networks did not deem worthy of telling their viewers was that Berri had been responsible for *eight* hijackings before the TWA incident; that he had called for suicide attacks on the withdrawing Israeli army; that he personally commanded the Amal militia, which had mercilessly slaughtered Palestinian women and children in Sabra and Shatila; that during the hostage crisis his militiamen killed two Palestinian nurses who had stumbled on the hostages' hiding place; and that neither Amal nor any other armed group could make a major move in Lebanon without Syrian approval.

One of the most revealing incidents during the crisis, which inadvertently exposed the inner workings of the media's bias, occurred on CNN. In the words of Tom Shales:

CNN showed its taped pictures from Beirut Saturday as an "unedited satellite feed," meaning no producers or editors had gone through the footage before it aired. Viewers may have been confused, or infuriated, at the zeal with which CNN reporter Jim Clancy baited hostages to condemn or at least implicate Israel in the crisis. He badgered the hostages on this point; he wouldn't give up until they agreed with his thesis that Israel was not justified in detaining its 735 Lebanese captives.

When asked about this episode, CNN anchorman Bernard Shaw said, "It was a mistake to show unedited material." Indeed it was, for it revealed the process by which propaganda is made to masquerade as news. An edited version would very likely have shown hostages "spontaneously" spouting anti-Israel statements, without any help from the friendly, objective, even-handed correspondent.

The correspondents were by no means the only players in this drama. Anchormen and talk-show hosts served the hijackers even better. One of the primary purposes of terrorist acts is to draw world attention to their "cause." Mindlessly serving this purpose, every network invited the most virulent anti-Israel spokesman available to "explain" the hijackers' grievances. The list reads like a Who's Who of the Arab lobby—James Abourezk, Jesse Jackson, Michael Hudson, Walid Khalidi, Clovis Maksoud, Hisham Sharabi, David Sadd, James Zogby, et al., not to mention the obligatory appearance on practically every major program of Said Rajaie-Khorassani, the Iranian Ambassador to the UN. Not surprisingly, all advocated yielding to the hijackers' demands—not, of course, because they approved of the act, but because one had to understand the grievances behind it. All agreed that terrorism could not be stopped until those grievances were eliminated, and all agreed that the only way to eliminate them was to cease supporting Israel. Only once did a television host, Ted Koppel, ask a guest, former Senator James Abourezk, if he thought it proper to discuss American foreign policy at such a time.

After the hostages' release, some anchormen and talk-show hosts were asked why so much air time had been given to the hijackers and their apologists. The reply was that the American public needed the education, and that it was fair to give the hijackers' point of view a hearing. On July 10, Tom Wicker of the New York *Times*, echoing this view, wrote in his column: "Was television 'used' by Amal? Of course, just as it is being used all the time by the Reagan administration for its own purposes." Here we have the ultimate evenhandedness: a "godfather" of cutthroats, kidnappers, and assassins linked with the democratically elected President of the U.S. One wonders how Wicker would have responded to a question asked of ABC anchorman Peter Jennings by Larry King, host of a CNN talk show: "Would you have let Hitler come on the tube in September 1939 to explain the reasons for the Nazi invasion of Poland?" Jennings adroitly evaded the question. (King's burst of common sense was unfortunately short-lived; two days later he had Allyn Conwell on his show for a whole hour, and treated him with perfect sycophancy.)

Perhaps the weirdest spectacle of all was the round of self-gratulation on a post-hijack program on *Nightline*, in which all the senior ABC correspondents in Beirut participated. Not only had they done no wrong, they smugly agreed among themselves, they had probably advanced the cause of peace and justice in the Middle East by exposing the defects of American policy there. The climax came when Charles Glass, a journalist whose good relations with the Shiites had enabled him to score several scoops during the crisis, said, "This ordeal is not over until the last Shiite prisoner in Israel is freed." Host Ted Koppel, with obvious embarrassment, hurriedly added, "and of course the seven American hostages still in captivity in Lebanon."

One irony of this entire story is that the Lebanese Shiites do indeed have legitimate grievances, grievances that have nothing to do with Israel or the U.S. They have been savaged, raped, and murdered by the PLO (the erstwhile darling of the media), exploited by Sunni Muslims, patronized by Christian Arabs, and oppressed by Syrians. Since they are the largest sect in Lebanon, it would have worked in their favor had they chosen to associate themselves with the democratic West. But instead, they have aligned with the fundamentalist Khomeini and the radical Assad. Perhaps their perception that the West is in decline has had something to do with this choice, if so, the media's glamorization of their anti-Western, terroristic behavior can only reinforce their contempt for us.

It is difficult to fathom why journalists side with fanatics and terrorists. Partly, perhaps, the reason may be sheer, abysmal ignorance: ABC-TV correspondent Michael Lee, reporting from Israel, once said, "I am standing here in what used to be independent Palestine." Then there is the palpable ideological bias among many journalists who grew up in the 60's and who still believe that every self-styled "liberation movement," especially if it is anti-American, must be good, no matter how fascistically it may behave. Too, there is probably some truth in what Jody Powell, once President Carter's press secretary, has written: "The mistakes and excesses of journalists are not primarily a product of ideological or partisan bias . . . the root of the evil is the love of money which translates into competition for ratings." In this particular hostage crisis, the "Stockholm syndrome"—the feeling, common among hostages, of gratitude and sympathy to their captors for not committing *worse* atrocities—seems to have affected newsmen in Beirut and New York as well.

Perhaps the special situation in Beirut provides still another explanation. Two weeks before the hijacking David Blundy, correspondent for the London Sunday *Times*, described the atmosphere of fear and intimidation in Beirut: "Many reporters have been withdrawn because of the risk of being kidnapped or killed. Those who remain find it increasingly difficult and dangerous to work." Another reporter told Blundy, "If we print atrocity stories, we will get a bomb through our window."

But whatever the reason or reasons for the conduct of the media in the hostage crisis of 1985, there is no doubt that it was they who were responsible for propagating and legitimizing the Orwellian idea that the real blame for the hijacking and the kidnapping lay less with the terrorists who committed these crimes than with the United States for supporting Israel—and most of all with Israel itself.

PRIME TIME TERROR[4]

The contour of the story is, of course, still familiar: the hijacking of TWA Flight 847 by Shiite terrorists, the demand that Israel release 700 of their comrades, the threats to kill the hostages, the quick deterioration in relations between Washington and Jerusalem and the subsequent patch-up job. The images, too, are probably still fresh: the pictures of the Boeing 727 stranded on the runway at Beirut International; the faces of weary, frightened Americans speaking to reporters, choosing their words carefully, surrounded by grinning thugs; the Shiite warlord, "Justice Minister" Nabih Berri, leering uneasily into the cameras; and all those talking heads on our television sets, spewing out an endless stream of "expert" advice. But some significant details of the story are perhaps already fading from memory, some of the specifics may already have been forgotten. There are things we should remember.

Specifically, we should remember Robert Dean Stethem, 23, of Maryland. He was six feet tall; he had dark hair and a dark mustache, a strong young man who enjoyed his work as a Navy diver. He was wearing a blue Hawaiian shirt and light blue cotton trousers on the last day of his life. "They dragged him out of his seat, tied his hands and then beat him up," sixteen-year-old Ruth Henderson told reporters in Algiers and London. "I watched as they kicked him in the head, then they kicked him in the face and kneecaps and kept kicking him until they had broken all his ribs. Then they tried to knock him out with the butt of a pistol—they kept hitting him over the head but he was very strong and they

[4]Reprint of an article by Micah Morrison, Israel correspondent for *The American Spectator*. *American Spectator*. 18:12+. S. '85. Copyright ©1985 by *The American Spectator*. All rights reserved. Reprinted by permission.

couldn't knock him out." At the end, they stuck a pistol behind Robert Dean Stethem's right ear and blew him into oblivion. His body was dumped on the tarmac at Beirut.

Specifically, we should remember the removal of those, as the media rather delicately put it, "with Jewish-sounding names." It was "the most terrible moment" of the ordeal, said one of the women from Flight 847. It reminded her of the selections at Auschwitz. "They were looking for Jews or Israelis," another passenger said. After the passports had been collected, "I heard them calling those passengers one by one: 'You, come here! You come here!' . . . They pushed them off the plane." One of those selected turned to his fellow passengers as the terrorists led him away. "Don't forget us," he said.

Specifically, we should remember the way a small band of professional killers brought the government of the United States of America to its knees for a few days, temporarily drove a wedge between Washington and its firmest Mideast ally, and turned an all-too-willing world media into the bootlicking lackey of international terrorism. It is important to keep these things in mind, not to let them fade into the amnesic haze brought on by next week's horrors, the next hijacking or bombing or famine or massacre or war. There are lessons to be absorbed from the murder of Robert Dean Stethem and from the echo of Nazism implicit in the selection of the "Jews," lessons to be learned about the nature of Mideast conflicts, about the use and abuse (and non-use) of American power, including the technological power of the communications industry, and about our options for the future.

Without question, the hijackers of Flight 847 were professionals. These were not the teenage suicide commandos who drive truck bombs into army posts and embassies, knowing they will go straight to the Gates of Paradise for their glorious acts of martyrdom. (In fact, recent reports from the area indicate that many of the car bombers are aligned with secular, pro-Syrian terror groups. The popular view in southern Lebanon has long been that the young kamikazes are more fired up on drugs than religious fervor when they make their last drive, and that pledges of substantial Syrian-provided financial reward to their families are a strong factor in convincing them to commit suicide.) In many ways

Flight 847 represents a perfect case of air piracy: Athens Airport was used because of its lax security and proximity to Beirut; the plane was kept moving to thwart any quick, early rescue attempt; fresh men were brought in to relieve the hijackers; women and children and the elderly were removed from the plane—holding these types of hostages has very negative PR value; a young man was murdered, just to show that the boys meant business; and then the hostages were scattered through a tightly guarded area, effectively ending any chance for a rescue. The hijackers made all the right moves.

In contrast, the Americans seemed to be making all the wrong moves during the first critical hours and days of the crisis. On the operational level, Washington's Delta Force counterterror outfit simply wasn't close enough to the action. If it were stationed in the Mediterranean region it could, theoretically at least, have mounted a lightning strike against the plane when it first touched down in Algeria. Unless the terror war moves to North Carolina, there's not much sense in stationing Delta Force at Fort Bragg.

But it was at the diplomatic level that the Americans seemed to exceed all natural bounds of incompetence, while in Jerusalem bewildered Israeli officials tried to make sense of U.S. intentions. A small part of the snarl was due to plain bad luck: The most trusted and informed American in Israel, U.S. Ambassador Sam Lewis, had just wound up a lengthy tour of duty, leaving matters in the hands of his relatively inexperienced second-in-command. Yet the base treatment of Israel can hardly be laid at the doorstep of the American Embassy in Tel Aviv—it was Washington that for the first ten days of the crisis led Jerusalem through a crossfire of mixed signals and ambiguous statements. Anger and confusion—was this any way for an ally to act?—began to mount.

"The United States does not know what to do with itself," wrote the center-right daily *Yediot Aharonot* on June 18, four days after the hijack. "It is deterred by Algeria, which blocked U.S. access to the plane; it fears the hijackers' leader, a minister in the Gemayel government; and it is wary of an operation against the hijackers. . . . The U.S. is pinning all its hopes on little Israel to rescue her. If the United States took some action and asked us for assistance—that would be one thing. But to shirk all responsibility and to quiver through and through in hiding while uttering a silent prayer to Israel to bear the entire burden of rescuing the Americans—this is going too far. . . . This approach will ultimately hurt America more than Israel."

Less than a week into the affair, the view from Jerusalem, expressed in numerous "background" comments and journalistic fulminations, was that the White House was tacitly encouraging the American media to put "unofficial" pressure on Israel to release the 700 prisoners. The Israeli media began to run stories about the negative impact of the hostage crisis on U.S. public opinion regarding the Jewish state. Jerusalem tried to calm the situation by instructing its diplomats in the U.S. to turn down all interview requests for the time being.

Israelis were, by and large, dismayed by the American double-dealing. "A cat and mouse game is being played between the United States and Israel," Gideon Samet wrote in the prestigious and, by Israeli standards, rather stuffy center-left *Ha'aretz* newspaper. "The American government has avoided requesting the release of the Shiite prisoners in order not to look as though it's capitulating to terrorism. Israel, justifiably, is awaiting a formal, high-level request before making a decision. This is a situation without precedent in the close friendship between Israel and the U.S. It stems from the special circumstances surrounding the hijacking, but there is also a confluence of frustration between two countries which, over the course of several years, have lost their capacity for deterrence. Having been burned in the past, they're reluctant to take action now."

The commentator pinned the Israeli loss of a "capacity to operate" on the results of the Lebanon war, which he compared to an "enormous rescue operation" in which the army was sent in to "free an entire country from the hands of PLO hijackers." Heavy casualties were sustained in that three-year operation and Israel today is a country traumatized by its still-fresh wounds. America's weakness, in the *Ha'aretz* writer's view, an opinion echoed elsewhere in Israel during the crisis, stems from the Iranian hostage debacle. "The American hostages in Tehran who returned the day President Reagan was sworn in (they were freed in exchange for the release of Iranian deposits in American banks) returned as a symbol of the government's failure to rescue them through different means. America's military pride had already been trampled in the Iranian desert in an embarrassing operation. Since then, Washington has been wracked by the nightmare of weakness in its battle against terror. . . . Conservative American experts and past government leaders (Kissinger, as usual) expressed their belief that the U.S. will overcome its weakness and will do 'something' . . . but that is just wishful thinking about restoring America's capacity to use its strength."

The "official" Israeli response to American waffling came in some characteristically blunt comments by Defense Minister Yitzhak Rabin in an interview with ABC. Rabin was prime minister during the dramatic rescue of the Air France passengers at Entebbe. In a long and distinguished career in the Israeli army and government, Entebbe is said to be the event Rabin is most proud of—and it was his pride and reputation as one of the tough heroes of Entebbe that was severely battered when, less than a month before the TWA hijacking, he released more than a thousand convicted terrorists in exchange for three soldiers held by a splinter faction of the PLO. Rabin was hurt by the storm of criticism over the swap. The old soldier wasn't about to be lured into appearing weak again.

"Look," he testily replied to the questioner, "let's not play games. . . . If there is a request on the part of the United States [for the release of the Shiites as part of a deal to free the TWA hostages] please come out and say it. . . . The problem is an American problem. The hostages are Americans. They were caught on board an airline which carries the United States flag. The United States government has to make up its mind: What do they want to do? It's first and foremost their decision. I've never tried to avoid responsibility. I've never shrugged off my shoulders the need to make a decision as a prime minister and now as a defense minister, facing terror acts against Israelis. I expect the United States to do the same."

The Israeli press reported that Rabin's remarks "astonished" Secretary Shultz and "angered" President Reagan, but the substance if not the style of delivery was welcomed in Jerusalem. After all, the tactlessness of Rabin's statements did not detract from their truth: The hostages were Americans and they were flying under the protection of the U.S. flag. Once again, America was appearing paralyzed by indecision, and to make matters worse it was slipping into a cowardly and half-hearted attempt to shift some of the responsibility.

Whether as a result of the Rabin flare-up or not, within a few days—by Day 10 of the crisis—officials of the two countries finally got their act together. Letters of mutual support were exchanged, and Israeli officials kindly floated the suggestion that the American wavering was due to the confusion of "mid-level personnel." The left-wing *Al Hamishmar* newspaper reported that the "current trend" in Jerusalem was toward "maximal coordination" with Washington. The crisis was winding to a close. Thirty-one Shiites were released from the Israeli jail at Atlit— government spokesmen insisted that the release had nothing to do with the terrorists' demands, a transparent piece of nonsense— and within a week the Savior From Damascus would step in and the hostages would be winging their way home.

Viewed in relation to the Washington-Jerusalem diplomatic axis, the TWA episode demonstrated the need for better emergency communication channels and procedures. A temporary news blackout and high-level consultations early in the game could have prevented many of the problems that arose between the allies. Viewed, however, in relation to the terrorists and their unwitting accomplices, a news blackout was the last thing they wanted. Jimmy Dell Palmer, the hostage with the bad heart released midway through the crisis, laid his finger right on the pulse of terrorism when he told a radio reporter in London that "the Shiites have achieved their goal. They wanted publicity. They got it."

Boy, did they get it. The world media, and particularly the U.S. television media, transformed little Nabih Berri and the Shiites into major players on the international stage, proving again to terrorists and potential terrorists everywhere that the disgraceful rapaciousness of ratings-hungry television executives and sycophantic TV reporters will guarantee that, at minimum, the messages of terrorism's often sick and twisted causes will gain worldwide attention if a dramatic incident is arranged, media access furnished, and sufficient "color" provided. "You should not be surprised that Americans are still thought of as innocents abroad," an Israeli security official who served in Lebanon told me. "Look at the behavior of your television crews. They run around searching for a story. They hand out more money than many poor Arabs get from a year's work. Suddenly every illiterate Shiite carrying an assault rifle is appearing on the news all over the world. Of course the terrorists are going to prolong the crisis—they are absolutely delighted by all the publicity."

So the world media, allied with Shiite terror, provided a public relations platform that beamed messages to the Western world. Yet the TWA hijacking served another important purpose directed toward the Arab, not the Western, world. For weeks prior to the hijacking, Berri's Amal militia and its allies had been slaughtering Palestinians in the refugee camps around Beirut. The Shiites want to prevent the return of the hated PLO to a position of power in Lebanon. (Oddly enough—or not really so odd when you consider the menacing undercurrents of the Mideast—preventing a PLO return is also a goal shared by Syria and Israel.) The fighting around the camps triggered an angry reaction in many parts of the Arab world, including efforts to convene an Arab League summit to condemn Amal. Kuwaiti newspapers, in a view coinciding with the opinions of some experts in Israel, charged outright that Amal commissioned the hijacking to divert attention from its massacre of Palestinians in the camps. Berri pulled a neat switch here. He not only deflected attention away from the camps, but also gave the media a "good guy" image to play off the nasties holding the plane. Berri was portrayed as a sort of white-hatted Lebanese cowboy riding to the rescue of unfortunate Americans held hostage by mysterious extremists. The total lie was swallowed by many people, although anything more than a cursory glance at a few facts available early in the affair would have indicated something of the degree of Amal's involvement. There was, for example, the hijackers' original demand that four suspected terrorists held in Spain and Greece be released immediately. All four men are or were known members of Amal. There was also the report from several sources identifying the two hijackers as former bodyguards of—guess who?—none other than the minister of justice himself, Nabih Berri.

Some things in Lebanon never change. Whether it was Berri's Amal or one of the dozens of sicko groups operating out of the slums of Beirut that actually pulled off the hijacking, it's clear that Berri cynically manipulated the situation and then, when the hostages departed for Damascus, went back to the pressing business at hand—slaughtering the Palestinians.

Ironically, one of the biggest Arab killers of them all, Hafez Assad of Syria, won much American praise for his "constructive and helpful" role in freeing the hostages. Although there are conflicting opinions about whether Syria had a hand in initiating the hijacking, it certainly could have stopped it sooner. Shiite and other terrorists train in "Terror Academies" in the Syrian-held Lebanese Bekaa Valley, and although the schools are controlled and funded by Iranians working out of the Iranian embassy in Damascus, the area is completely under the thumb of Syrian Intelligence. Nothing moves in or out without Syrian approval. Praising Assad for help in the fight against terrorism is like praising a rabid dog for keeping cats out of the neighborhood. This is the man who ordered the assassination of Lebanese President Amin Gemayel's brother and Druse leader Walid Jumblat's father when they got in his way, who ordered the murder of at least ten thousand citizens in the Syrian city of Hama when the Moslem Brotherhood began to chafe under his dictatorial and corrupt rule, who has imprisoned and tortured untold thousands of Syrians, and who—in an event little noticed during the TWA affair—welcomed an Iranian delegation that had just signed a pact with Libya pledging to terrorize "moderate" Arab countries, annihilate Israel, and strike at U.S. interests in the Arab world.

Indeed, warning signs of a new terrorist offensive are appearing all over Lebanon. "Various terrorist groups are organizing in preparation for future action on a broad scale," cautioned the respected and well-informed military commentator Ze'ev Schiff in *Ha'aretz*. Schiff reports that the Syrians have arranged meetings for the Iranians with extremist Shiite and Palestinian groups in Lebanon, that links between pro-Syrian Palestinians and Shiites are becoming stronger, and that Yasir Arafat is desperately trying to get his al-Fatah men back into the country. The Iranians, writes Schiff, "are investing funds in extremist groups among both the Shiites and the Palestinians, with the motto that all Moslems must organize for the great war against Israel." Arafat, for his part, and despite all the sound and fury about diplomatic initiatives, cannot allow his control of a dwindling PLO to be further diminished by the dramatic terror acts of others—to remain a player among Arab warlords, Arafat must keep his terror options open. Thus the April 20 attempts to land more than twenty al-Fatah terrorists on an Israeli beach. The Israeli navy intercepted the ship and sank it. Prisoners captured in the operation told of being personally briefed by Abu Jihad, one of Arafat's top aides, who ordered them to kill as many people as possible. On other Mideast terror fronts, the underground war between Syria and Jordan and their respective surrogates seems to be heating up, with bombings and assassinations in the Arab world and Europe; car bombings and ambushes continue to plague the Israelis in their narrow security zone on the Israel-Lebanon border; on the Golan Heights, several sabotage incidents have been attributed to a hostile Druse organization; and in Egypt there are numerous reports of a new upsurge in Islamic fundamentalism.

What can be done about threats like this, about terrorism that emanates from no one central source? Tying a yellow ribbon around the old oak tree is not part of the solution; indeed it may be part of the problem in that it sends the wrong message to terrorists. It signals a naive, spineless America, an America that dwells in an atmosphere of appeasement, helpless when confronted by the hooded face of an unknown enemy.

The answer lies in action, intelligent and forceful action. If the United States is serious about stopping terrorism it should go past the rhetoric of "war on terror" and actually, legally, make a formal declaration of war. In a war you pay the tragic price today with the certainty that tomorrow will be better. How much danger would we face now if the United States and Israel had mounted a commando raid on the TWA jet on the second day of the hijacking, with the simultaneous bombing of selected targets in Beirut, the terror training camps in the Bekaa Valley, the Iranian embassy in Damascus, and terror bases in Libya and South Yemen? A sophisticated, superbly coordinated show of massive force would put a very clear message across: Strike at us once and we will go to the ends of the earth to destroy you.

In a war you impose censorship, which in this case would deny the enemy propaganda outlets. In this respect the media barons in the U.S. might be shamed into borrowing a page from the Israeli book and forming an editors' committee that would exercise voluntary censorship. How much terrorism would there be if the major media institutions agreed to give terrorist incidents only, say, a one-minute spot against a black background on the nightly news, and agreed to bury the story back on page five in a somber, black-bordered box?

It would help, too, if America stationed its counter-terror troops where they are needed. The logical place is Israel. The country has the most experience in dealing with terrorism, it is technologically advanced and strategically located. Much was said in the closing days of the hostage crisis about the special relationship between the United States and Israel, but terrorism drove a wedge between the two allies once and it could do so again. Next time—and there most certainly will be a next time—we must be ready to strike hard and fast. Terrorism has already declared war on democracy, and in this most unusual of wars the democratic nations are going to have to use some pretty tough tactics to fight back. We have no choice. Our future depends on it.

IV. FIGHTING BACK

EDITOR'S INTRODUCTION

The history of the American encounter with terrorism began in the early days of the Republic, when American merchant ships were attacked by pirates operating out of the Barbary states of Algiers, Morocco, Tunis, and Tripoli (in present-day Libya). The U.S. government paid tribute and ransom to the Barbary pashas for years under a series of treaties and twice went to war over flagrant violations.

The experience of the United States with the Barbary pirates foreshadowed its twentieth-century experience with their modern counterparts. The difficulties of prevention, deterrence, negotiation, and retaliation have multiplied with the growth of a global economy and the rise of powerful and antagonistic ideologies. In a completely homogeneous world—the world to which Soviet Communism, for example, aspires—there would be little room for terrorism.

Proposing countermeasures to terrorism has become a national pastime since hijackings, bombings, and hostage crises became regular features of the nightly news. In the first selection, a *Newsweek* article offers ten practical recommendations for keeping international terrorists at bay and making it harder for them to carry out their exploits. In the second, reprinted from the *Department of State Bulletin*, Abraham Sofaer outlines a plan for strengthening international conventions for the prosecution and extradition of terrorists and for the sharing of intelligence. The third selection, excerpted from a symposium printed in *This World*, presents the views of a number of scholars, writers, and policy makers on how to prevent and combat terrorist attacks, including evaluations of the use of force.

Though the authors in this section make a variety of recommendations, one thing is certain: without a greater understanding of the history of terrorism, government officials responsible for establishing national policy will make little progress against it. The investigation of the suicide car bombing that killed 241 Marines in Lebanon in 1983 concluded that top officials in the Reagan administration and the military did not know much about past terrorism in the Middle East. Ignorance about other areas of the world has often been cited as a cause of America's failure to grasp the political realities of those areas and to anticipate troublesome developments. The attempt to learn the truth about the rest of the world—and about the consequences of U.S. foreign policy—is at the root of self-defense against terrorism.

TEN WAYS TO FIGHT TERRORISM[1]

1. Crack Down on Unsafe Airports

Recently Business International Corp., a consulting firm for multinational companies, published a list of the world's 10 most dangerous airports. Athens and Beirut—the two airports involved in the Flight 847 seizure—are at the top. The others are in Karachi (where saboteurs have blown up two airplanes in recent years); New Delhi (where Sikh extremists pose a danger to travelers); Manila (where the airport shares a runway with a Philippine air base that could become a target for antigovernment rebels); Teheran, Iran, and Tripoli, Libya (where officials have harassed and detained passengers arbitrarily); Conakry, Guinea; Lagos, Nigeria, and Yaoundé, Cameroon (where overzealous bureaucratic controls hamper security efforts). Governments in all these countries should be pressured to make their airports safer. If they fail to change, governments and airlines should start boycotting the worst airports.

Beirut airport should be shut down altogether—at least until the Lebanese government can reassert control over it. Right now,

[1]Reprint of an article by Mark Whitaker and *Newsweek* bureau reporters. *Newsweek*. 106:14+. Jl. 1, '85. Copyright © 1985 by Newsweek Inc. All rights reserved. Reprinted by permission.

it has become a sort of 20th-century pirate base. Armed militia-men control the airport, and authorities refuse to search them or their bags. Few of the metal detectors and other security devices work. Already this year there have been five hijackings in Bei-rut—not counting Flight 847. The Muslim authorities who con-trol West Beirut oppose closing the airport; they argue that it would penalize civilian travelers and favor Lebanon's Christians, who want a new airport built in their half of the city. Ordering the U.S. Navy to crater the runway might constitute an act of war; it would also take a quasipermanent offshore naval presence to en-sure that the runways weren't rebuilt. But the United States could begin by considering ways to destroy the runways anyway—if only to goad the Lebanese to police the airport first.

As for the other airports, it may be enough to threaten them with loss of passengers and money. Last week Ronald Reagan ad-vised U.S. citizens against flying to Athens. Within days Greek civil-aviation authorities agreed to allow airlines to retain separate security procedures—a practice the Greeks had recently decided to ban. They also agreed to allow a team of specialists from the Montreal-based International Air Transport Association (IATA) to visit the airport and review security operations. If Washington issues similar warnings about other airports—by posting lists in U.S. embassies around the world—the authorities who run them may be shamed into action. If they aren't, more drastic measures should be considered—including legal penalties against travel agents who book passengers through the worst airports.

2. Tighten Airport Security

Although X-ray scanners in airports do a good job of inspect-ing luggage, they are too easy for sophisticated terrorists to cir-cumvent. Wherever possible, airports should install state-of-the-art security equipment—including three-dimensional scanners and detectors that can spot plastic explosives and pick out suspi-cious bottles as well as weapons. Authorities in Israel, West Ger-many and Switzerland have perfected other techniques that should be employed more widely; they include the double-checking of bags, using dogs to sniff luggage and searching passengers by hand. The Israelis also question passengers—often twice, to try to catch them in a lie. It may ultimately be necessary to eliminate carry-on luggage. All checked luggage should be X-rayed, to guard against time-release or remote-control bombs. No passengers should be exempt from searches. Right now it is too convenient for terrorists to slip weapons onto planes with ground-crew members, diplomats and other VIP's who are rarely checked.

More attention should be paid to the people who carry out security procedures. Sociologist Allan Mazur of Syracuse University points out that airport employees are like nuclear power plant operators: their jobs are often highly sensitive but also tedious and tiring. To make sure that security personnel are alert, terrorism specialist Robert Kupperman of Georgetown University's Center for Strategic and International Studies (CSIS) suggests that airports rotate them more frequently and test them periodically by trying to sneak weapons past them. Airports should also consider paying their security staffers more—in order to attract the best people possible.

Tighter security should extend to transit lounges. At present, even many security-conscious airports don't insist on searching passengers in transit. But that makes it easy for a terrorist coming from a country where security is lax to slip weapons onto a continuing flight. Most airport terminals are also vulnerable—a fact demonstrated again last week when a bomb ripped through the Frankfurt Airport. France's Comité de Sûreté is considering one way of dealing with that problem: installing video cameras in airports. But Rodney Wallace, director of facilitation and security for the IATA, maintains that that may not be enough. He argues that it may eventually be necessary to keep everyone except passengers with tickets out of terminal buildings.

The usefulness of President Reagan's proposal to put armed federal marshals aboard U.S. flights is less clear. Two of the world's safest airlines—El Al and Swissair—assign armed guards to their most sensitive flights. But the measure is not a guarantee against terrorism: a Jordanian Boeing 727 that was hijacked in Beirut on June 12 had eight sky marshals aboard. This option would also be very expensive—and dangerous. Stray bullets from a gun battle between terrorists and sky marshals could penetrate the wall of the plane and cause the cabin to decompress; they could also sever electrical lines or puncture fuel and hydraulic lines and start a fire. For that reason, Kupperman argues that ways should be investigated of arming sky marshals with weapons that can't penetrate a plane's fuselage. Given the plan's drawbacks, Kupperman has another sensible suggestion: that Washington start by concentrating the sky-marshal program on particularly dangerous routes in the Middle East, North Africa and Southern Europe.

3. Protect Terrorist Targets

After the bombings of two U.S. Embassy buildings and the Marine barracks in Beirut, Washington has finally gotten serious about beefing up security at its diplomatic posts around the world. Secretary of State George Shultz has asked Congress for an additional $236 million in 1985 to improve security at the State Department and at 13 facilities overseas. There are plans to create computerized Marine control booths, to spend $20 million for barriers and to allocate another $4 million in rewards for information about terrorists. More barricades, buffer zones, explosive-sniffing dogs and bodyguards would all help. Congress should appropriate the money quickly—then follow up to make sure that it is being spent wisely.

The fact that no U.S. facility is safe was underlined again in Washington last week. A young man carrying a gun walked into the State Department and went to the seventh floor. He shot his mother, a secretary to State Department counselor Edward Derwinski, then killed himself. The State Department stressed the shooting was not a terrorist incident. But later it announced that from now on, guards will check all cars coming into the State Department parking lot. Security officers will also insist that anyone without an employee identification card pass through newly installed metal detectors at the entrances to the building.

4. Expand Intelligence Gathering

Good intelligence has always been the best way to beat terrorists. In the 1970s the United States and Israel managed to thwart numerous attacks in the Middle East by penetrating the Palestine Liberation Organization. More recently, the Italians and the West Germans have all but shut down the Red Brigades and the Baader-Meinhof gang by turning members of their cells and getting them to testify against their comrades. "They've done a spectacular job in reducing violence," says former CIA Director William Colby. "They've shown that although you can't eliminate terrorism totally, you can reduce it to a residual level."

As terrorism in the Middle East has increased, however, U.S. intelligence in the region has grown weaker. The fall of the shah of Iran, the splintering of the PLO and the collapse of the Lebanese Christian Deuxième Bureau have deprived Washington of valuable sources of information. The CIA's top Mideast analyst, Robert Ames, was killed in the 1983 bombing of the U.S. Embassy in Beirut; so were 35 other agents, including some of the agency's most experienced "controls." Secrecy has been compromised by what one former CIA director acidly calls the "I've got a secret" syndrome—the desire of agents to show how important they are by leaking intelligence operations to the press. The new Shiite terrorist groups—Islamic Holy War, Hizbullah and Al Dawa Islamiya—have also "compartmentalized" themselves, not allowing their terrorists to know what others are doing. That has made it difficult for the CIA to get information even from those few Shiites it has managed to debrief.

Still, Washington must not give up the intelligence battle. By relaxing post-Watergate constraints on domestic intelligence gathering, the Reagan administration has helped the FBI to achieve greater success in neutralizing terrorist threats. Now, according to knowledgeable officials, the administration has a plan to recruit and train Arab agents to infiltrate suspected terrorist groups in Lebanon, Syria and Iran. So far Reagan has yet to sign the necessary "finding" for this Intelligence Support Activity (ISA)—partly because his intelligence agencies are fighting about who should run it. But as a first step toward restoring U.S. intelligence capabilities in the Mideast, those agencies should stop squabbling—and Reagan should approve the ISA.

Congress will still have to keep an eye on the CIA to prevent abuses. As recently as March, an informal attempt to implement

Washington's new infiltration policy dramatized the dangers of supervising hired agents. According to administration sources, the CIA recruited former members of the Christian-run Lebanese intelligence service to investigate terrorist activities in Lebanon. Then, acting on their own, some of the agents planted a car bomb in a Beirut street in an attempt to kill radical Shiite religious leader Sheik Muhammad Hussein Fadlallah. The group missed Fadlallah but killed 92 civilians. And according to sources in Beirut, leaked reports of the foul-up in the American press helped incite the terrorists who hijacked TWA Flight 847.

5. Train for Trouble

The Reagan administration should do more to prepare diplomats and officials who might find themselves in the midst of a terrorist crisis. British cabinet ministers and civil servants frequently engage in elaborate crisis games, including exercises with their elite commando squad, the Special Air Service (SAS). But U.S. officials have been reluctant to follow suit. "There seems to be more of a machismo attitude here," says Kupperman, "that we don't need to prepare in that way for managing a crisis." Despite the difficulties in freeing up time, these war games should also involve the highest-level people in the government. "No mid-level person is going to be in charge when a crisis breaks out," Kupperman emphasizes. "We have to get a regular program of crisis gaming going, and we have to make sure that at least cabinet-level people are involved in it."

Among other things, war games would help give presidents a better sense of their military options. Chalmers Johnson of the University of California at Berkeley points out that Jimmy Carter had never visited the Fort Bragg base of the U.S. Army's Delta Force team until after it failed to bring off the Iranian rescue mission. Johnson ventures that Reagan hasn't inspected the Delta Force, either. If U.S. officials had done more advance planning in the Iranian situation, they might have reached different conclusions about Carter's rescue raid. Soon after the seizure of the U.S. diplomats in Teheran, the Israeli army war-gamed possible rescue operations. The Israelis concluded that the only feasible commando action was to mount a surprise raid on Qom, kidnap Ayatollah Ruhollah Khomeini—and offer a trade for the captive Americans.

6. Improve International Cooperation

It is easy to be cynical about international counterterrorism agreements. More than 100 countries—including Lebanon—have signed the Hague treaty of 1970, which calls for punishing or extraditing hijackers, but many fail to observe it. When they do, however, it can make a difference. "The moment Fidel Castro started sending people back to the United States," points out Wallace, "hijackings to Cuba stopped."

Washington and other capitals should swallow their skepticism and keep trying to make cooperation work. They should make a greater effort to follow through on existing agreements, such as the Hague accord and a 1978 agreement between the United States and its allies to suspend air services to countries that harbor hijackers. President Reagan should also be supported in his proposal for an international task force to combat terrorism. Possibilities include multinational commando units, international penalties and jails for hijackers, even antiterrorist tribunals. If possible, such agreements should also be kept informal—to maintain secrecy and maneuvering room.

7. Negotiate Flexibly

Officials need to think harder about how to handle a terrorist crisis once it is under way. In this area, specialists have mastered a number of tried-and-true tactics. Patrick Dalager, head of the Law Enforcement and Security Training Division at Texas A&M University, stresses the importance of choosing the right negotiator—ideally someone who speaks the terrorists' language, understands their history and culture, is street-smart but also a good listener. Former national-security adviser Zbigniew Brzezinski points out the desirability of winning concessions early in a crisis, before positions on both sides harden. A third rule is to attempt to establish a relationship of trust with hostage-takers. A fourth is to wear terrorists down, depriving them of sleep by talking to them round-the-clock and forcing them to haggle over minor demands such as food and water.

But if the current crisis has demonstrated anything, it is that terrorists have learned to anticipate these stratagems. To keep U.S. negotiators off balance, the hijackers of Flight 847 kept flying back and forth between Beirut and Algiers. To make sure they didn't get worn out, they brought aboard additional armed gunmen. Finally they took the hostages off the plane so that responsibility for guarding them could be shared. Now U.S. officials have to figure out new ways to defuse these counterploys. To keep planes on the ground during a hijacking crisis, it may be necessary to shoot out their tires or to refuse to refuel them. Officials should also think about ways of sealing off skyjacked aircraft, so that terrorists can't bring comrades aboard or take hostages off.

It may not be wise for officials to declare publicly that they will not make concessions to terrorists, as Reagan has done from the start of this crisis. Such statements may sound principled and tough-minded, but they constrain efforts to carry out the bargaining that inevitably takes place with hostage-takers. "I disagree with the statements that have been made about no negotiations," argues Colby. "The fact is that any government will negotiate, if not directly, then indirectly."

Reagan has done a better job, however, in demonstrating another maxim for dealing with terrorists: don't create an atmosphere of panic. In retrospect, even former Carter administration officials concede that their president made a mistake with his strategy of immersing himself in the Iranian hostage crisis at the expense of everything else. "Adopting the right attitude is important," says Iran expert Gary Sick, a National Security Council staffer under Carter. "It must appear he [the president] is going on with other business, not letting this crisis interfere with the normal running of the country. The right thing to do is . . . to make it clear that it's up to others, like Nabih Berri, to resolve the thing. Otherwise, the president is made to look impotent, as though he's being yanked around by terrorists." Sick adds that maintaining a business-as-usual profile may not help free hostages any faster. But he points out that it doesn't hurt negotiations, either.

8. Don't Rule Out Rescues

For any U.S. president, saving the lives of innocent captives should always be the first priority during a hostage crisis. Even so, Reagan may have made a mistake in publicly foreclosing the use of military force as long as negotiations were continuing. Holding alive the option of a rescue mission keeps terrorists guessing—and may encourage them to make concessions more quickly.

But if the rescue option is to be effective—either in practice or as an incentive to deal—it must be credible. U.S. officials insist they have "a very good capability" to carry out attacks like the Israeli raid on Entebbe or "in those kinds of circumstances." But the United States is a long way from the areas where most terrorist incidents occur. And given the growing sophistication of hijackers, the hours lost in getting the U.S. Army Delta Force to the scene from its base at Fort Bragg, N.C., may also mean lost opportunities. One step toward making the rescue threat more convincing could be to station special-operations units closer to the Middle East and other hot spots of terrorism. The units would need training facilities there to maintain their skills—and still keep their activities secret.

9. Lean on Terrorist Allies

The United States and its allies should search for ways to penalize countries that assist and harbor terrorists. Once a crisis has started, they should begin, as Reagan has done, by persuading friendly countries in the region to condemn the perpetrators. Then they should send back-channel signals to adversaries who might have an influence over the terrorists.

One option available for putting indirect pressure on Iran in particular is to offer U.S. support to Iraq in the gulf war. Yet that proposal is fraught with problems. Not only would American aid take a long time to get to the Iraqis, but supporters of Israel would be sure to fight such a move. It could also play into the hands of Moscow. Until a few years ago, Iraq was firmly in the Soviet camp; only recently has it begun to make overtures to the United States. If Baghdad patched things up with Moscow, the Soviets would benefit enormously from an Iraqi victory over Iran. "Completely destabilizing Iran now is not in our interest," argues one U.S. official. "We have nothing going there and the Soviets would have the upper hand in whatever the next phase may be."

Another possibility under active consideration in Washington is an attempt to quarantine Shiite areas of Beirut. "West Beirut and the southern suburbs are a cesspool that ought to be dealt with," says one administration official. Such a quarantine might involve dispatching U.S. Navy ships to blockade Beirut, shutting down the airport and eventually even sending in ground troops. Edward Luttwak of Georgetown's CSIS goes so far as to propose blockading the entire Lebanese coast. Once Beirut is sealed off from Syria and the Syrian-controlled Bekaa Valley, Luttwak argues, U.S. forces could use photographs and other intelligence to track down the hijackers of Flight 847. "Care should be taken to reconstruct the identifications of these people and their leaders," says Luttwak, "and we should then hunt them down no matter how long it takes." Some even advocate assigning hit squads to kill the terrorists—but assassinations violate American values and are against U.S. law.

Less extreme forms of pressure are also available. One source in Beirut suggests that Washington urge friendly Persian Gulf states to deport their Shiite immigrants. Most gulf states would be glad to comply, since they fear the threat of Shiite fundamentalism. And deportations from the gulf would deprive the Shiites of a vital source of income. "This would really hurt the Shiites," points out the Lebanese source, since they depend on money sent home by relatives working abroad. Kupperman suggests that if Arab terrorism keeps up, the Reagan administration might also seek a U.S. federal court injunction against major banks that make petrodollar transfers to countries that either abet terrorists or refuse to condemn their deeds. Such a move would cause an uproar in the banking industry and may therefore have little chance of approval. But given the extent of America's economic influence around the world, U.S. officials and businessmen should be thinking about ways to bring that power to bear in fighting terrorists.

10. Order Selective Reprisals

For more than four years Reagan administration officials have been threatening to strike back at terrorists. But each time an opportunity for reprisals has come, they have hung back, stressing the complexities of finding targets and complaining about the difficulties in getting the Pentagon to agree to a retaliatory raid. Now U.S. officials should begin to see that this combination of tough talk and toothless response carries dangers of its own. As terrorism expert Brian Jenkins of the Rand Corporation says: "Threats of retaliation that aren't carried out create unfulfilled expectations that lead to the conclusion that America is impotent. It also encourages other terrorist groups, who begin to realize that this can be a pretty cheap way to wage war on the United States."

Administration officials are currently reviewing a list of retaliatory measures they might take after the Flight 847 hostages are released. The options include bombing Hizbullah barracks in the Bekaa Valley, hitting Islamic Holy War safe houses and training camps in eastern Lebanon and striking at terrorist hideouts and arms caches in Beirut. Other potential targets are power plants, refineries and the Kharg Island oil terminal in Iran; Iran's Bandar Abbas naval base, Bushehr air base and Revolutionary Guard training centers, and Libyan terrorist camps at Zawia, Ras Hilal, Sirte, Sebha, Tajjuna and Misurata. If the administration is serious about striking back, it must come up with a plan that would have a reasonable chance of taking out specific terrorist targets without causing too great a risk to innocent civilians.

No one should overlook the dangers of retaliation. It will fuel anti-Americanism in the Middle East. It will increase the odds that terrorists will strike in the United States (although that may be a danger, anyway). It may also have only a limited deterrent effect, serving more to help Americans shed their sense of helplessness than to put an end to terrorism. But at the very least, it would show that U.S. officials mean what they say. And that is always a crucial message to convey to terrorists.

As long as terrorists remain at work, skeptics will recite reasons why the United States and other democracies cannot hope to defeat them. They will stress—quite rightly—that terrorism often has roots in deep-seated political grievances, and that the cycle of violence cannot be broken until those grievances are addressed. They will argue that societies like the United States, which put a premium on liberty and the highest value on human life, will always be vulnerable to bomb throwers and airplane hijackers. The doubters will also conclude that it is impossible to ensure success against fanatics who are eager to blow themselves up and win a ticket to heaven. But those are only reasons for combating terrorism cautiously—and without illusions. They are not reasons for giving up.

FIGHTING TERRORISM THROUGH LAW[2]

The timeliness of today's session is painfully obvious. We have just emerged from another harrowing encounter with terrorism in Lebanon. The hijacking of TWA #847 is one in a rash of recent terrorist atrocities. Seven Americans and other innocent civilians remain in the hands of kidnappers in Lebanon.

Less than 1 month ago, nine civilians and four off-duty U.S. Embassy guards were gunned down at a sidewalk cafe in San Salvador. Over 300 men, women, and children were killed when an Air India flight disappeared mysteriously not far from here. A bomb put on another flight in the same Canadian city almost simultaneously exploded in Japan, killing two baggage handlers and injuring many others. A bomb in the Frankfurt airport during the same week killed two and injured several more. And a delicate, brilliantly executed investigation by Judge Webster's Federal Bureau of Investigation saved Prime Minister Rajiv Gandhi from what might well have been the same fate his mother met some months ago.

Even more sobering is the realization that the timeliness of today's topic was predictable. Ask yourselves when, during the last 10 years, this topic would have lacked tragic immediacy. Just 9

[2]Address before the American Bar Association by Abraham D. Sofaer, legal advisor to the U.S. State Department, July 15, 1985. *Department of State Bulletin.* 85:38–42. O. '85.

months ago, Prime Minister Thatcher narrowly escaped injury when a bomb planted by the Provisional IRA [Irish Republican Army] exploded at her hotel in Brighton, killing 4 and injuring 34. In July 1983 after repeated PLO [Palestine Liberation Organization] attacks, a group of Jewish extremists fired randomly at Arab students at the Islamic College in Hebron, killing 3 and wounding 33 others.

The State Department has estimated that, from 1979 to 1983, 2,093 people have been killed as a result of international terrorist incidents and 4,349 injured. We can be grimly certain that, if this subject is set again for next year, we will have new tragedies to talk about.

Of course, nothing we say today, or do tomorrow, could put an end to the evil that is modern terrorism. As long as people find it in themselves to torture and murder indiscriminately, to advance their political ends, we must live with terrorism in its many manifestations. And we are not about to witness any fundamental change in human nature or the sudden enlightenment of mankind through a divine will.

Indeed, a common thread among most terrorists is the deep belief each holds in the justice of his cause. Each hears, or pretends to hear, his own particular god cheering on the sidelines as he kills and maims the innocent—be that god Jehovah, Allah, Marx, a utopian vision of society, or some insane dream of racist supremacy.

Controlling domestic criminality is itself an endless challenge, even though every civilized nation has criminal laws prohibiting antisocial conduct, national police forces universally empowered to use reasonable and necessary force, and courts with authority to punish violators. In the international arena, while we have conventions, agreements, and customs that make many terrorist acts universal crimes, international practice and doctrines greatly limit the enforceability of these norms. Furthermore, we lack anything like an international police force to apply rules of conduct or courts routinely to enforce them through punishments. Even when we can lawfully apply force against terrorists, its utility is often limited by the value we attach to human life.

The problem also has a political dimension. While a consensus can usually be found among the citizens of particular nations against terrorist acts, on the international scene, as President Reagan noted last week, a number of states either provide safe havens for terrorists or actively encourage terrorism and use terror as a weapon in their war against free governments.

The TWA Incident

You can best appreciate the special difficulty of dealing with international terrorism if we review some of the issues the U.S. Government has faced during the latest crisis. The underlying facts are no doubt familiar to you all.

Three Lebanese hijackers flew from Beirut to Athens where two of them boarded TWA #847 bound for Rome. The third man was unable to get a seat on the plane and was subsequently arrested in Athens. Shortly after takeoff, the hijackers produced pistols and grenades, commandeered the plane to Beirut for refueling, and then took it to Algiers. They demanded that their coconspirator in Athens be reunited with them in exchange for the release of the Greek nationals on the plane, and the Greeks agreed. The plane was then flown back and forth between Beirut and Algiers. In the process, all but 39 passengers and crew were released. On the ground in Beirut, the hijackers mercilessly beat and then shot to death Robert Stethem, a young U.S. Navy diver. They were then joined by members of both Hizbollah and Amal forces, who took a dozen passengers off the plane for "safekeeping." The hijackers sought publicity and got it. The world was treated to a media extravaganza that gave tastelessness new meaning.

The immediate problem posed by the hijacking was to get back the hostages safely and in a manner consistent with our overall security interests. President Reagan and Secretary Shultz set the rules for our conduct: no deals, maximum diplomatic pressure, and the use of reasonable, discriminate force, if necessary. Their efforts succeeded without further loss of life. We continue to seek the return of all other hostages in Lebanon.

In addition to obtaining the safe release of the passengers and crew, we are working to achieve four additional objectives: to bring the hijackers to justice, to get back the plane, to end the routine use by terrorists of the Beirut International Airport, and to improve security at the Athens airport. We are also seeking to rally like-minded governments to join us in improving worldwide safeguards for civil aviation security.

The Hijackers

You will recall that one of the hijackers was arrested at the Athens airport. As a party to the Tokyo, The Hague, and Montreal conventions against terrorism, Greece had the responsibility to hold the would-be hijacker until he was extradited or prosecuted. Instead, Greek officials swapped the terrorist for the Greek nationals on the plane.

Releasing the hijacker in exchange for some of the hostages was a grave mistake. The reason no exception is written into the obligation to extradite or prosecute aircraft hijackers is simply that, once one begins to make exchanges with terrorists, there is no end to the types of deals they would demand. Kuwait, to its credit, has repeatedly resisted terrorist demands that it release convicted terrorists. We have insisted that Greece abide by its obligation to hold alleged hijackers until extradition or prosecution. As you will see, however, we can do little more on this issue until the conventions are made enforceable.

By signing The Hague and Montreal conventions, Lebanon agreed to extradite or prosecute terrorist hijackers. In addition, customary principles of international law support the principle that pirates must be punished either in the requesting or requested nation. Under legislation passed last fall, the TWA hijacking is a crime under U.S. law. We have filed a formal demand that Lebanon fulfill its international obligations to take law enforcement measures against those responsible for the TWA hijacking and the crimes they committed; Attorney General Meese will determine when to file a formal demand for extradition and what other law enforcement options to pursue.

The press greeted with skepticism our intention to pursue the hijackers through legal means. They questioned the point of such an effort, and if the Government of Lebanon cannot control its airport, how can we reasonably expect it to investigate, identify, arrest, and prosecute the individuals responsible for the hijacking?

The short answer to this is that we cannot know in advance that an effort to arrest the hijackers is bound to fail. Lebanon is a complex place, and if the news stories are accurate—that an effort to arrest them is being made—a good result could come about through circumstances we cannot now entirely anticipate.

In any event, Lebanon's inability to arrest the offenders cannot relieve it of its obligation to try and to keep trying until it succeeds. Our effort to bring these hijackers to justice has significance far beyond the individual case. We must persist in asserting that the rule of law be obeyed, if we want to retain the hope that some day it will be obeyed.

Don't let this discussion mislead you. If Lebanon or Greece refused to carry out their obligations under the antiterrorism conventions, our prospects for enforcement would be slight. Thus far, neither the conventions nor customary law have been held to create enforceable duties. Parties to the conventions have repeatedly refused to extradite or prosecute hijackers and, indeed, have supported their activities. Kevin Chamberlain, a legal counsellor of Britain's Foreign and Commonwealth Office, wrote of the conventions in a recent article that "there is no effective means of ensuring compliance with their provisions."

Frustration over the refusal of several nations to comply with the antihijacking conventions led the economic summit seven to issue a "declaration" at Bonn in 1978. In it, the seven codeclarants, whose airlines account for about 70% of all civil aviation, "jointly resolved that their governments should take immediate action to cease all flights" connected with any country that "refuses extradition or prosecution of those who have hijacked an aircraft and/or do not return such aircraft. . . . " Thus far, the declaration has been invoked only once—against Afghanistan in 1981. On that occasion, moreover, the sanction was imposed only after the declarants had given Afghanistan the 1-year notice, argued by some to be required by bilateral aviation agreements.

If the hijackers are not brought to justice, we will be faced with the option of seeking action under the Bonn declaration. However persistently we pursue this course, it is a difficult one, depending on the will and courage of seven nations, each with independent interests and views.

Let me depress you further with the fact that, even when a hijacker is arrested, that is no assurance he will be brought to justice. Many states will not extradite their own citizens, or will extradite them only for the most heinous crimes. A state that does not provide for the death penalty under its laws may refuse to extradite a person for an offense that could be punished by death in the requesting state, or it might condition extradition on assurances that the death penalty will not be imposed.

An especially important obstacle to extradition is the so-called political-offense exception found in the extradition law of many states. As interpreted by the U.S. courts, this exception prohibits the extradition of any person whose crime, however serious, was committed in the course or in furtherance of civil war, insurrection, or political commotion. Invoking this doctrine, American courts have refused the last four extraditions sought by the executive branch of IRA members guilty of murdering police and military officials. France has refused to extradite Americans to the United States on this basis, where they claimed to have committed their criminal acts for political reasons, including alleged racial oppression. Of course, a refusal to extradite loses its sting if the requested nation prosecutes the offender but no enforcement mechanism exists to insure that a prosecution will occur, that a meaningful sentence will be imposed and served. And these obstacles, I hasten to add, describe only a few of the difficulties in bringing hijackers to justice.

The Plane

TWA's aircraft remains on the ground at Beirut International Airport, although Article 11 of the Tokyo convention states that the "contracting state in which the aircraft lands . . . shall return the aircraft and its cargo to the persons lawfully entitled to possession." Article 9 of The Hague convention imposes a similar obligation, and the Bonn declaration applies to a nation's refusal to return a hijacked plane.

We are assisting TWA in getting back its plane. The risks associated with using an American crew have complicated the situation. Here, too, the Government of Lebanon claims it is willing to comply with its obligation, but the absence of effective control over the airport has posed substantial obstacles.

Athens and Beirut Airports

Immediately after the hijacking, we took steps to insure that our concerns about security at both the Athens and Beirut airports were made known to the traveling public. Athens airport has been the object of special scrutiny on security grounds for many years, not only by the United States but also by other governments. Deficiencies there had been associated with other terrorist acts, including the hijacking of TWA #847. Given the history of repeated incidents, the issuance of a travel advisory became imperative. The Greek Government has objected to this measure, claiming it to be unfair and discriminatory. We acted reluctantly, however, and only because prior efforts to improve security by Athens had been unsuccessful.

International law obliges all states engaged in international civil aviation to insure adequate security at their airports. In 1974, ICAO [International Civil Aviation Organization] adopted annex 17 to the Chicago convention on international civil aviation, establishing standards and recommended practices on security. That document has been amended and updated several times as experience warranted, and it is a useful benchmark against which to measure the sufficiency of security standards at airports. We believe, moreover, that when experience demonstrates that special circumstances at a particular airport require more stringent measures than those recommended by ICAO to provide necessary security, those measures must be adopted. Our travel advisory was also a lesser remedy than is expressly authorized by the U.S.-Greece bilateral aviation agreement, which provides for the suspension of all air service for unsafe conditions.

Material improvements have been made at Athens airport, and we are working with the Greek Government to bring about the necessary improvements. The Secretary of State looks forward to being able to lift the advisory at Athens, consistent with his obligation to protect American citizens abroad from unwarranted danger.

Long before the hijacking, the Department of State had advised U.S. citizens that the unstable conditions prevailing in Lebanon made travel through Beirut airport unsafe. In fact, the Beirut airport has been involved in 36 separate terrorist hijackings in recent years. After the latest incident, President Reagan determined [pursuant to Section 1114(A) of the Federal Aviation Act] that Lebanon was acting inconsistently with the Hague Convention for the Suppression of Unlawful Seizure of Aircraft and suspended the rights of all U.S. air carriers to engage in air transportation, direct or indirect, to and from Lebanon, as well as the rights of Lebanese carriers to engage in air transportation to and from the United States.

In addition, Transportation Secretary Dole took actions modifying the authority of Middle East Airlines [MEA] to fly to the United States and prohibiting the sales of air transportation to, from, or through Lebanon [pursuant to the Federal Aviation Act, Sections 404 and 403]. We are encouraging like-minded countries to join in these efforts, which we intend to continue until that airport is effectively secured against use by terrorist groups.

The government of Lebanon has objected to these measures, claiming it should not be punished for what it could not control. But it is precisely Lebanon's lack of control that justifies the measures we have adopted. Until Lebanon assumes control, it is our obligation to discontinue air commerce involving that airport. We are ready to cooperate with Lebanon in accomplishing this objective as quickly as possible. Meanwhile we have demonstrated our willingness to allow flights to the United States by Lebanese aircraft, so long as they do not use the Beirut airport. For example, flights of an MEA-leased aircraft between Cairo and New York have not been terminated.

Lebanon also claims that our actions violate the U.S.-Lebanon bilateral aviation agreement. That agreement, like most other aviation bilaterals, requires that disputes be settled through consultation and arbitration and provides that it can be terminated only after 1 year's notice.

150 The Reference Shelf

We are confident that the measures taken with respect to the Beirut airport are consistent with our bilateral aviation agreement with Lebanon and with our obligations under international law. Air traffic is conducted either without enforceable traffic rights, on the basis of comity and reciprocity, or under bilateral agreements often containing safety and security provisions. Both types of bilateral arrangements complement the basic multilateral framework for international civil aviation, the core of which is the Chicago convention. This multilateral framework places a high priority on the safety of international civil aviation and incorporates, as requirements, the ICAO standards for aviation security and other air terrorism conventions. A specific reference to these ICAO standards is included in Article 6 of the bilateral agreement with Lebanon. Sound commercial practice suggests that acceptable standards of safety and security for aeronautical facilities are an essential precondition to the operation of this network of aviation rights. They are, therefore, an essential element of the consent of a state to be bound to a bilateral accord.

Furthermore, under established principles of international law, an international agreement, such as a bilateral aviation accord, may be terminated or suspended when a provision essential to its object has been violated or when fundamental conditions underlying it have been changed. The concepts of material breach and fundamental change of circumstance, *rebus sic stantibus* [incorporated in Articles 60 and 62 of the Vienna Convention on the Law of Treaties], can be invoked by parties to bilateral aviation agreements when air safety and security violations warrant. In cases of urgency, these actions can be taken promptly, without notice periods [as Article 65(2) of the Vienna convention reflects].

International law also allows proportionate actions in connection with agreements, in response to breaches of related legal duties. Whatever the provisions of a country's particular bilateral aviation agreement, almost all participants in international civil aviation are party to the Chicago convention, with its airport security standards, and to the air terrorism conventions. The duties of countries under these accords are owed to all states and to the traveling public. Lebanon's conceded inability to insure the minimum degree of safety necessary to permit air transportation services with other countries deprives it of the capacity to insist upon the exercise of reciprocal commercial air rights.

Our bilateral agreements should explicitly provide that air services may be suspended in response to violations of fundamental international obligations. A number of our agreements, including the one with Greece, specifically authorize us to enforce the ICAO standards bilaterally by suspending operating rights. But not all agreements contain such a provision, and most fail to incorporate violations of the Tokyo and The Hague conventions as express grounds for suspending operating rights. We need to reexamine all of our agreements, to urge other nations to do the same, and to take steps to insure that future ones provide for more effective enforcement of international air safety and security obligations. A tight web of such agreements would be a powerful incentive to countries to abide by their solemn commitments to fight terrorism and to insure aviation security.

Conclusion

I am sure that some of you are thinking at this point: Forget about law; let's just go in there and get the killers. And if we can't find them, let's punish the crazed groups to which they belong until they stop harming innocent persons.

The President has warned terrorists and the states which support them that our patience has run out. They had best heed his warning. International law recognizes the right to use force in self-defense against armed attacks. The groups that are responsible for attacking us in Lebanon, El Salvador, and elsewhere have openly announced their intentions to keep on trying to kill Americans. To the extent that they are state supported, or beyond the capacity of their governments to control, we are entitled now to use necessary and proportionate force to end such attacks. This Administration's willingness to use appropriate force in itself has a deterrent and moderating effect on our enemies.

But the possible use of force should not distract us from the role that law can play in this struggle. The President flatly rejected any improper use of force. We cannot become terrorists, he said, in the fight against terrorism.

While force will play its part, the President challenged us last week to develop "a better domestic and international legal framework for dealing with terrorism"—to "deal legally with lawlessness." And we stressed the need to move our focus from the tactical to the strategic and to recognize the international pattern of terrorist activity.

The President has called us to the highest duty lawyers can have. He has asked us to fight, within the constraints of our moral values and legal traditions, an enemy that scorns and exploits our respect for those limiting rules. The inadequacies and obstacles to meaningful legal action against hijacking which I have reviewed today should have demonstrated that we have a great deal of difficult and frustrating work ahead of us.

• We have to create meaningful enforcement mechanisms, through both bilateral and multilateral arrangements, for the obligations stated in antihijacking conventions and in the ICAO standards.

• We need to amend the Bonn declaration to provide for a range of sanctions and for their swift imposition whenever any important aspect of the aviation conventions is violated.

• We must strive to overcome the reluctance even of civilized nations to extradite terrorists. In this connection, we have made important, recent progress. We just signed with the United Kingdom an amendment to our extradition treaty which will eliminate the political-offense exception for major crimes, such as hijacking and murder. The ABA must join us in seeking Senate confirmation of this important step against terrorism; the gun is not a proper substitute for the ballot box in free societies which offer fair systems of justice.

• We must continue to encourage all like-minded nations to join us in our efforts. One of the most heartening developments of the latest crisis is the cooperation and support we received from virtually all nations, including the United Kingdom, Canada, and Israel, but particularly from concerned Arab states. Almost all the Arab nations condemned the hijacking and murder; Jordan's King Hussein called it the work of mad dogs. Syria and Algeria played constructive roles in helping to get our hostages back, and President Assad may continue to demonstrate good will by helping us retrieve those who remain captives in Lebanon.

• We must organize ourselves more effectively to deal with terrorism by treating international law enforcement as a routine aspect of foreign relations. We will use, in this effort, our new authority to issue rewards for help in bringing those who attack Americans to justice.

• We must get ahead of the terrorists in technology. Just as we have adopted a Strategic Defense Initiative, we need a terrorist defense initiative that enables us to detect and defuse terrorist threats before they can do damage.

The fight against terrorism through law will take ingenuity, endurance, and money. We must harness the outrage we feel over these acts to give us the strength to carry on the struggle. When you start to tire, I suggest you think about the innocent victims of terror, including young Robert Stethem. A passenger on the plane described Stethem's screams as the kind that went on until the very breath went out of his lungs. The thought of those screams will keep me in this fight for as long as it takes to prevail.

TERRORISM—WHAT SHOULD WE DO?[3]

William V. O'Brien
Professor of Government, Georgetown University

As often happens with controversial terms, "terrorism" is seldom explicitly defined. Terrorism is war of a kind and it may be used as a subordinate strategy within wars that otherwise follow traditional military patterns. Terrorism's uniqueness lies in its use of armed force against targets that would be exceptional or aberrational in regular warfare, with results that have little to do with traditional military necessity. Terrorism is usually carried out by small groups, directed against targets chosen for their potential shock effect rather than their military utility. Its purpose

[3]Excerpted from a symposium of scholars, writers, and policy-makers concerned with terrorism. *This World.* p 31+. Fall '85. Copyright © 1985 by The Institute for Educational Affairs, Inc. All rights reserved. Reprinted by permission.

is to create an environment of fear, apprehension and loss of confidence in the existing security systems so that they are weakened and likely to collapse.

Terrorists attack two kinds of targets: random individuals and groups and, alternatively, persons and places having high symbolic importance as representative of "the system," for example, high officials, police, successful businessmen, important public places. Successful attacks against these two kinds of targets leave the message, in the first case, that no-one is safe; in the second, that "the system" is doomed. These attacks are accompanied by two kinds of demands. The first type of demand may require release of political prisoners, payment of ransom, granting political and economic concessions. The second kind of demand advances the utopian revolutionary agenda of the terrorists. If the first type of demand is met, more of the same will surely follow. The second kind of terrorist demand constitutes an unacceptable ultimatum.

Accordingly, giving in to terrorist demands is generally futile and self-destructive. You cannot do business with terrorists. You must either fight them or turn the other cheek.

Walter Laqueur observes, in his book *Terrorism*, that a fundamental characteristic of terrorism is its violation of established norms. Even war has norms that survive despite their frequent violation. The only norm for terrorism is effectiveness in terrorizing. The international law of war requires that belligerent forces identify themselves, carry arms openly and observe the law of war. Principal among the laws of war are the principles of discrimination or non-combatant immunity and proportion. Whereas strategists use the term "collateral damage" for injury to non-combatants and non-military targets, moralists and international lawyers speak in terms of the principle of discrimination or non-combatant immunity from direct intentional attack. They also prescribe the principle of proportion of ends and means.

Terrorists do not distinguish non-combatants or "innocent people" from the generality of the society they are attacking or from its armed forces. Two rationales usually inform their strategies and tactics. The very fact that the victims of terrorist attacks are, and are considered to be, innocent third parties enhances the shock effect of attacking them. Alternatively, the terrorist may decree that everyone living in a certain society is guilty of its sins and deserving of punishment, for example, infants only grow up to be imperialist oppressors so they are fair game.

Terrorists may attack military and internal security forces but the essence of their strategy is to attack what would normally be considered non-combatant and non-military targets by means violative of the minimal requirements of the law of war. In contemporary strategic terms, they wage countervalue rather than counterforce war, to the extreme.

The principle of proportion is to be found among military principles as well as in the moral doctrine of just war and in the international law of war. It counsels the avoidance of unnecessary damage in war. This principle, however, does not fit terrorist strategy. Disproportionate damage is inflicted for shock effect and justified by the referent of utopian necessity.

As earlier observed, terrorism as a strategy can be adopted as the sole policy of a small group or it can be incorporated into the array of strategies of a larger force. The Irish Republican Army is a small terrorist organization whose sole military instrument is terrorism. The Viet Cong was a revolutionary/guerrilla organization that used countervalue terror extensively but also engaged in counterforce guerrilla warfare as well as occasional conventional operations. The Palestine Liberation Organization (P.L.O.) occasionally gives the appearance of aspiring to regular counterforce military capabilities but relies overwhelmingly on terrorism.

Counterterrorist strategies can be active or passive. However, defensive strategies can seldom contain terrorism satisfactorily. Some form of deterrence seems to be essential in the war against terrorist attacks. Air travel can be made more secure. Prominent terrorist targets such as diplomats and embassies, important businessmen and their homes, justice, police and military officials, and the like can be provided enhanced protection. Public places can be rendered less vulnerable by such expedients as controlling luggage and packages in train and bus stations and in popular meeting places. Internal security forces can improve counterterrorist intelligence and with it break up terrorist organizations and activities.

Still, after all such necessary efforts have reduced the vulnerability of possible terrorist targets, some terrorist attacks will nonetheless succeed. The critical question that has the United States government and the American public in a quandary is what to do when the terrorists succeed. Two forms of reaction have been employed by other societies victimized by terrorism, particularly terrorism that emanates from foreign countries. The first is case by case retaliation. Each time the terrorists inflict damage, damage is inflicted in return on the terrorists and/or those who support them. The other form of reaction is sometimes called preemptive but is normally more properly described as preventive.

The retaliatory response, often called a reprisal, follows an antecedent terrorist attack or series of attacks and is linked implicitly or explicitly to the terrorists' action. Such retaliatory attacks have as their rationale punishment, the infliction of retribution on the terrorists and their supporters. They also serve to satisfy an outraged society's demand for retaliation. Retaliatory attacks linked to previous terrorist acts are easier to justify legally and morally than preventive measures against terrorists. They tend to reassure domestic opinion. Mere retaliation, however, has seldom provided a sufficient answer to terrorism. Reactive reprisal raids leave the initiative in the hands of the terrorists who can always reduce the pace and intensity of the hostile interaction if things seem to be going against them.

Preemptive action anticipates imminent terrorist attacks. True preemption of terrorists is conceivable but unlikely. What is more feasible is preventive action aimed at the sources of terrorist operations. Over time it should be possible to locate the principal bases from which terrorists organize and carry out their operations. They may be camps and quasi-military installations or they may simply be localities in which the terrorists merge with the local population. These bases and support areas may be attacked in preventive strikes, much as an army attacks an enemy's staging areas. To be effective, preventive strikes should be sustained with a view of inflicting serious long-term damage on the terrorists and their infrastructure. They should not be viewed as responses to particular terrorist attacks although such attacks may provide good occasions for pressing preventive counterterrorist operations.

I call such counterterrorist attacks preventive/attrition since they are designed to wrest the initiative away from the terrorists, make them defend themselves at times, places, and at a pace and intensity chosen by the counterterror forces.

In both retaliatory and preventive/attrition strikes three overlapping targets are envisaged. First, the terrorists themselves and their infrastructure are the primary target. However, if the terrorists are operating from a foreign country, as is so often the case, the sovereign state and/or *de facto* controlling power that either supports them or acquiesces in their presence and terrorist activities is considered a target. Finally, the population in the immediate vicinity of the terrorists' base is made to pay the price for its complicity in terrorism, whether voluntary or coerced.

Attacks on the latter two targets have thus far been eschewed by the United States with rare exceptions. On December 4, 1983, U.S. Navy planes attacked Syrian antiaircraft missile and gun batteries, ammunition supplies and radar installations in three locations in Lebanon following Syrian fire on U.S. Navy F-14 reconaissance planes. While not directed at the terrorists who had attacked U.S. forces on a peace-keeping mission, notably in the October 23, 1983 suicide bombing in Beirut that killed 239 Marines, this retaliatory operation was related to counterterrorist tactics because of the need to guarantee U.S. overflight of the area. Otherwise, the U.S. retreated from the terrorists' challenge by not attacking suspected terrorist bases in the Bekaa Valley or elsewhere, in areas clearly under Syrian control, as the French did on November 17, 1983. Nor was the United States willing to risk the collateral damage involved in attacking terrorist bases intermingled with a population that either supported or acquiesced in their activities. This pattern of unwillingness to confront states such as Syria and Iran and to inflict collateral damage on populations around terrorist bases has persisted through the recent aerial hijacking of TWA Flight 847 by terrorists sponsored or supported by Iran and Syria June–July 1985. Nevertheless, attacks on an international peace-keeping force can be considered terrorism. If such attacks were to be treated as acts of war, self-defense measures would be justified.

During the TWA Flight 847 hostage crisis President Reagan repeatedly emphasized that he would not order the use of armed coercion against the terrorists if substantial collateral damage would be involved. There was also a clear reluctance to confront and attack Syria or Iran directly. This was perhaps understandable while the release of the hostages was being negotiated. However, the longer term implications are that the United States does not dare punish states that sponsor and support terrorist acts against it and its citizens.

Moreover, unless consideration is given to weighing the lives of hostages in a particular situation against the credibility of the counterterrorist deterrence posture of the United States and the lives of other potential hijacking victims, the terrorists and their state sponsors will clearly win every round in what could be an escalating terrorist war.

Assuming that maximum efforts will be made to improve U.S. passive defense capabilities against terrorism, the heart of the matter is deterrence. Unlike nuclear deterrence, deterrence against terrorism must be made credible by actual demonstration of the actions threatened in the deterrence posture. Nuclear deterrence has made possible the avoidance of nuclear war, but there is no way that terrorism can be totally deterred. When terrorism occurs there must be an assured, effective reaction that imposes unacceptable damage on the terrorists and those who make possible and/or fail to prevent their activities.

Such retaliatory action in vindication of a counterterrorist deterrent posture must, as in the case of conventional and nuclear deterrence, involve the certainty of collateral damage—that is, of death and destruction of non-combatants and targets not related to the terrorists except as protective covering under which to hide and seek immunity. We contemplate collateral damage in conventional and nuclear war. There is no avoiding it in counterterrorist operations.

This does not mean that armed force should be used without regard to the principles of discrimination and proportion. Rules of engagement should reflect these principles. However, unless the United States is willing to risk the consequences of confronting

foreign powers that support anti-American terrorism and of taking responsibility for the minimal collateral damage involved in
hitting terrorists in their sanctuaries, no use of American armed
force will be possible unless the terrorists are so foolish as to isolate
themselves totally outside the jurisdiction of any state.

The alternatives are stark. A nation either decides to fight terrorism, in which case it must be willing to attack foreign sanctuaries as well as the terrorists themselves, or it becomes resigned
to rolling with the terrorists' punches and making ineffectual pro-
tests and pleas for collective action. If a nation waits for collective
action it will surely suffer the fate of the United States during the
Iranian hostage crisis, the Marine's ordeal in Lebanon, and the
1985 TWA hijacking. Collective action will not be forthcoming.
Counterterrorism ultimately requires self-help.

Resistance to terrorism, while critical, is not the sole vital interest of a nation. It is possible that in given situations such resistance must be deferred in deference to more important
considerations. But if the United States continues to build a reputation for turning the other cheek to terrorists, that cheek is going
to become very bloody. The heart of deterrence is manifest political will. Terrorism will not be deterred without it.

Robert Grant
Member of the Executive Group,
Policy Project on International Terrorism,
The Atlantic Council of the United States

In responding to the question of whether he ever aspired to be
"advisor to a Prince," Raymond Aron wrote, "I would have been,
in all likelihood, incapable . . . of taking or inspiring the decisions, often necessary, which send young men to war and to death.
Not that I oppose the use of force, in theory or in practice. But
it is one thing to acknowledge in the abstract the resort to arms,
and another to convince the President *hic et nunc* to have recourse
to them." The hijacking of TWA Flight 847 provided a particularly stark illustration of this dilemma of the "Prince" and his senior advisors.

Any American use of force during the event itself would have condemned all or most of the hostages to death. Foreclosing the immediate use of force, as the United States did, meant in effect some compromise of the enunciated principle not to negotiate with terrorists and inevitably rendered more difficult retribution and punishment of the hijackers. Besides the implicit promise not to retaliate that was made during the negotiations, American use of force after the hostages' release was further blocked by the detention in Lebanon of seven other Americans. Retaliation would have very likely threatened the lives of these and other Americans still in Lebanon.

While many terrorist incidents are not as dramatic and do not place on policymakers the same direct burden of responsibility for the lives of noncombatant citizens as hijackings and hostage incidents, all terrorist attacks share the characteristic of putting democratic governments under substantial political pressure. The loss of life resulting from terrorism has been insubstantial compared with fatalities caused by automobile accidents or, in the United States at least, even ordinary crime. Yet terrorism, either through the total randomness of its violence or through its selective targeting of particular groups and prominent figures of society, creates the enormous frustration for a government of not being able to provide for the security of its citizens, and undermines public perceptions of the government's ability to rule. Furthermore, successful overseas terrorist attacks diminish prestige and influence abroad.

Terrorism thus presents two kinds of challenge for democratic societies, one internal and the other external. Internally, terrorism must be effectively combatted without undermining the civil liberties that so fundamentally distinguish democratic nations from totalitarian ones. Italy and West Germany both confronted and surmounted this challenge during the 1970's. They succeeded in very sharply curtailing terrorist activities, and although certain police and judicial powers were expanded in the fight against terrorism, no one could reasonably argue that these nations became "police states."

Externally, the problem is one of how to combat terrorism while maintaining a sufficient regard for other foreign policy interests, including that of adhering to a different standard of international behavior than the one followed by the Soviet Union and its allies. The United States has hitherto been spared from serious domestic terrorism; the government has therefore largely focused within the last few years on how to counter international terrorism. The increasing involvement of states in direct support of terrorism through provision of safe havens, funds, training, and logistical support, and sometimes through direct sponsorship of terrorist attacks, has greatly heightened American concern over the international terrorist threat.

Obtaining increased cooperation from our allies and other friendly nations is one of the most often suggested methods in the United States for enhancing the effectiveness of international counterterrorism efforts. Senior administration officials have repeatedly emphasized that, in the words of Secretary of State George Shultz, "terrorism is an international problem that requires the concerted efforts of all free nations." Administration officials have most prominently stressed two potential advantages that international collaboration can offer in the fight against terrorism. First, timely intelligence is widely regarded as the key to combatting terrorism successfully, and international exchanges of intelligence information can obviously reinforce the capabilities of any one country in this critical area. Secondly, international cooperation can arguably provide credible diplomatic and economic tools for combatting terrorism that would be totally ineffective if employed unilaterally.

While there is undoubtedly room for increased efforts on the part of the United States and its allies in the area of intelligence sharing as well as that of collaboration between police and judicial authorities, the reluctance to apply diplomatic and economic sanctions against states that directly support terrorism has probably been the most frustrating aspect for the United States of allied attitudes towards antiterrorism cooperation. Apart from the use of military force, diplomatic and economic sanctions are seen as the only means of imposing penalties upon states for their support and sponsorship of terrorism.

The United States and its allies have collectively taken only two antiterrorism measures of any significance in the diplomatic and economic areas. An agreement reached at the Bonn Summit of 1978 requires the interruption of normal air links with any country that refuses to prosecute or extradite hijackers. This agreement led to sanctions against Afghanistan in 1982. And in 1980, E.E.C. nations supported the United States in imposing trade and economic sanctions against Iran.

Several factors have been responsible for this limited record. Divergent foreign policy, economic, and domestic political interests have often blocked vigorous collective reactions to state-supported terrorism. Although the United States has made a considerable effort to persuade its allies to impose sanctions against Libya, both Italy and France have indicated to Washington that a policy of "excommunicating" Libya would not be useful. France, Italy, West Germany, and even Great Britain all seek to maintain or improve diplomatic and/or economic relations with Libya. West European economic and foreign policy goals (France and Italy have been particularly interested in maintaining a "political dialogue" with Qaddafi) have thus outweighed any interest in attempting to pressure Qaddafi into lessening his sponsorship and support of international terrorism.

Similarly, the major West European powers have been quietly exploring the prospects for improved relations with Iran, despite the country's major role in support of international terrorism. Nor has the United States been immune to the experience of having other factors override antiterrorism concerns. Regardless of whether the United States Marine presence in Beirut was well-conceived or not, it was apparent that domestic political pressure played a large role in the very precipitous nature of the Marine withdrawal. More recently, President Reagan, in a major speech on terrorism given in the aftermath of the TWA hijacking incident, omitted Syria from his list of states that support international terrorism, despite the fact that Syria is one of the major offenders. He made this omission for foreign policy and humanitarian reasons (the desire for Syrian assistance in obtaining the release of the seven remaining American hostages in Lebanon).

The Western response to state-sponsored terrorism has also been made more problematical by the absence of conclusive evidence directly linking any state to specific terrorist acts. Much circumstantial evidence has existed, but the 1984 slaying of a British policewoman by a gunman firing from inside the Libyan Embassy in London constituted a rare occasion when a state was actually caught with a "smoking gun." The outrage was so blatant that a rupture of British-Libyan diplomatic relations became inevitable.

Finally, Western nations have generally not perceived international terrorism to be a highly significant threat. National measures have been fairly effective against internationally supported domestic terrorists, and to a somewhat lesser extent against international terrorists operating within Western borders. With some notable exceptions, most international terrorist acts committed in the West have been directed against non-Western targets, inevitably attenuating the reaction of the Western nation concerned. Statistics released by French security services in early 1985, for example, showed that only a small percentage of international terrorist acts committed in France from 1982 to 1984 were directed against French targets.

Among our allies, only France has suffered from substantial terrorist attacks in Third World countries. Not only has the United States borne the brunt of the terrorist threat in the Third World, but as one of the world's two superpowers, the United States is inevitably more concerned than its allies by the blows to national prestige and credibility and by the image of impotence resulting from successful terrorist attacks overseas. On the whole, America's allies have regarded the terrorist threat beyond national borders more as an irritant than as a major foreign policy concern. Herein lies one of the major causes of the United States' failure to obtain greater support from its allies for antiterrorism measures. To a certain extent, terrorism has become another item in the list of Third World issues on which the United States would like more support for its policies than its allies seem prepared to give.

As with these other Third World issues, the United States can attempt to obtain greater allied cooperation either through pressure, or through persuasion accompanied by some compromising of American preferences in order partially to accommodate allied concerns. The latter approach may not be successful, and indeed has often not been successful in the past. But a policy of trying to force allied cooperation may not work either, and runs the additional risk of straining an alliance which is still the United States' single most important military, political, and moral asset in the international arena. Great care should thus be exercised before the United States exerts pressure over issues which are not fundamentally related to the alliance's central objective of deterring a Soviet attack against a NATO member state.

These various difficulties are reflected in the declaration on terrorism issued at the 1984 London summit of the seven major industrial democracies. Although terrorism was a major topic of discussion at the summit, the aspects of the declaration related to sanctions against states that support terrorism were fairly anodyne. For example, the proposal that each country "review the sale of weapons to states supporting terrorism" even if taken seriously, could only have a limited impact since the summit nations essentially were not supplying weapons to these states in any event. (France has been selling limited quantities of arms to Syria, and several Western nations have supplied Iran with non-lethal military equipment.)

In light of this analysis, what steps should the United States take in order to enhance the possibility of using sanctions as an antiterrorism instrument? First, an examination should be made of the potential effectiveness of sanctions in combatting direct state support for terrorism. This is especially necessary since the efficacy of sanctions on other issues (South Africa, the Soviet grain embargo, Rhodesia) has been widely questioned. If a persuasive case were made that sanctions would have an impact in curtailing state involvement in terrorism, it could conceivably influence allied views. Secondly, since its allies are on the whole more dependent on foreign trade and their economies are for the most part in a more fragile state, Washington could explore possible ways of more evenly sharing the burden of economic sanctions.

By themselves, these American measures are perhaps unlikely to bring about substantially greater allied support for the application of sanctions, but they could help to prepare the way for more vigorous action in this area in the event that future developments create a heightened perception of threat on the part of the allies. It is doubtful, however, that the United States Government would seriously contemplate sharing the burden of economic sanctions, especially in view of the massive American trade deficit.

There is only a limited range of options available for countering international terrorism, and above all state involvement in international terrorism. These options all conflict to varying degrees with either foreign policy, economic or domestic political objectives. As Secretary Shultz has said, "Economic sanctions and other forms of pressure impose costs on the nations that apply them, but some sacrifices will be necessary if we are to solve the problem. In the long run, I believe, it will have been a small price to pay." It remains to be seen what degree of adherence this statement can gather, not only among America's allies, but also within the United States Government itself.

Martha Crenshaw
Associate Professor of Government,
Wesleyan University

A public opinion poll conducted by A.B.C. News and the *Washington Post* after the release of the TWA passengers held hostage in Beirut in June shows that the majority of the American people oppose the use of military force in retaliation for the hijacking. Even those people who do support retaliatory policies are less committed to the use of force if it risks escalating into a wider conflict. Yet during the crisis 53 percent of those asked felt that the United States should take action against Middle Eastern nations aiding terrorism.

The June hijacking crisis highlighted an issue that has become central to the foreign policy of the Reagan Administration: whether to respond to terrorism with military force. Government decision makers seem as divided on this problem as the American public. Ironically, the Department of State presses for a more vigorous response, while the Department of Defense is cautious. The debate recalls the dispute between Cyrus Vance and Zbigniew Brzezinski over the wisdom of the hostage rescue mission in Iran. Neither thought that the rescue would succeed. Vance concluded that only diplomacy was feasible until the hostages were no longer useful to Khomeini in his domestic power struggles. Brzezinski insisted on the redemption of American honor. In his view, a military strike against Iranian interests (Kharg Island, for example) would serve the dual purpose of ending America's humiliation and obscuring what he expected to be a failed rescue attempt. The Soviet invasion of Afghanistan, however, made military intervention on a large scale too risky.

The present contentious reevaluation of American policy is the result of changes in the international environment and in American policy conceptions. The calamities the United States has suffered in the Middle East have brought terrorism home in a way that numerous earlier hijackings and attacks did not. Although the United States has unfortunately provided roughly one-third of the victims and targets for international terrorism since its modern inception in 1968, our policy of no concessions (dating from 1972 and the original establishment of a State Department office for combatting terrorism) had rarely been tested. In the 1970's the demands that terrorists made when they seized American citizens, airliners, or embassies were most often directed against host governments. Now they are more likely to be made of the United States. Furthermore, the extent and destructive magnitude of the attacks the United States has suffered in the 1980's—the numbers of hostages, their brutal treatment, and the extent of casualties in bombing attacks—has made the threat of terrorism more visible.

But what values does terrorism threaten? Terrorist attacks do not damage the material capabilities of powerful nations; instead they affect self-esteem. Governments seem particularly compelled to respond to terrorism when it jeopardizes domestic authority or international prestige. For the United States, largely immune to indigenous terrorism, the reputation for power in international politics must now seem at stake. Terrorism is particularly humiliating and embarrassing because it defies the rules of the games of both war and diplomacy and because terrorist organizations are so absurdly miniscule in comparison to the power of the state.

Terrorism is thought to bring a loss of face; the more powerful the state, the more face it has to lose. American decision makers must also see the response to terrorism in terms of the exercise of a wider international responsibility of upholding the values and norms of the existing world order. How a nation answers a challenge, no matter how minor, shows the entire world, not just the terrorists, how the state will respond to the next threat. If terrorists can act with impunity, it is conceivable that other challengers may be similarly inspired.

The American public may not agree with this interpretation of the terrorist threat. According to the polls, few people think that the United States lost face in the recent hostage crisis. Most think that world opinion of American strength is unchanged. This attitude may be attributable to Reagan's skillful handling of the crisis. But it may also mean that terrorism is not the blow to prestige that decision makers such as Brzezinski assumed.

The Reagan Administration's sensitivity to the issue of terrorism is closely tied to the prevailing belief among top officials that most terrorism is sponsored by foreign governments, not independently motivated radical groups. The Iranian hostage crisis brought about a revolution in expectations about how governments should behave with regard to foreign nationals. It was a formative experience in the life of the present Administration. In the minds of many officials the issues of terrorism and Soviet aggression, particularly in Central America, are also inseparably linked. Terrorism is perceived as but one weapon in the arsenal of America's enemies in the global struggle between Communism and liberal democracy. It is difficult to reconcile the belief in a Soviet-inspired conspiracy with the perception of Iran as the major perpetrator of terrorism in the Middle East, since Iran remains resolutely anti-communist (if equally anti-American). Syrian support for extremist terrorism is more easily explained in terms of bipolar conflict, given Syria's relationship with the Soviet Union, but the conflict between Syria and the P.L.O. remains puzzling. Nevertheless, the preoccupation with state sponsorship elevates terrorism to the status of a serious threat to national security.

The prominence of the issue of using force also stems from more prosaic considerations. In the past several years the United States has developed its capabilities for military intervention in trouble spots abroad. After the success of the Israeli raid on Entebbe in 1976, most Western democracies promoted the establishment of specialized elite intervention units. West German elite troops replicated the Israeli triumph at Mogadishu in 1977. This forward momentum was abruptly halted with the tragic end of the American rescue in the Iranian desert in 1980. Yet this loss strengthened American determination to correct the defects in the system which made the Iranian rescue mission prone to disaster. This development culminated in the establishment of the Joint Special Operations Agency in 1984. The United States military now has the capability to intervene to free hostages or to retaliate against selected targets worldwide. The possession of such resources increases the temptation to use them. Yet the seductiveness of the military option seems to affect political rather than military decision makers.

In analyzing military response capabilities it is essential to remember that there are two different alternatives, tailored to different circumstances and with different policy implications. Hostage seizures present a classic dilemma for which military rescue missions were originally devised. Governments, caught between the alternatives of a humiliating capitulation to terrorist demands and resistance which cost the lives of the hostages, moved to intervene militarily. Such interventions were short-term and had limited objectives. Terrorists, however, adapted to this response. They sought sanctuary in territory the hostage governments (for it is really governments, not individuals, who are held hostage) dared not attack. Or they dispersed their captives so as to impede rescue. The threat of massive suicide bombings can also be seen as an innovation in terrorist tactics, possibly in response to strengthened government capabilities. Rescue missions lost their relevance to this new threat. The ambition of advocates of retaliation and preemption is to prevent and deter such deadly attacks through military force. What we see, then, is that terrorism and the response to terrorism evolve in an action-reaction pattern. The outcome is that governments are now considering an escalation from the limited rescue mission, designed strictly to free hostages unlawfully held, to punishment and retribution on a larger scale.

Military retaliation against terrorist organizations or against the states who sponsor or assist them is a tempting prospect. Passivity is frustrating and demeaning; like appeasement, it seems only to invite aggression. However, is the use of force to defend against terrorists a sound policy? A number of questions about the effectiveness of an offensive or "proactive" military strategy come to mind. The critique I will mount here against the use of force rests exclusively on practical rather than moral grounds, although questions can be raised on the latter score. For the moment let us restrict ourselves to asking whether the use of force is an expedient strategy.

First, to be effective, both preemption (striking first in order to prevent an imminent attack) and retaliation (reprisals to punish those responsible for an attack against one's interests and to deter future attack) must be discriminate. Knowing who was responsible and where to find them requires exceptional intelligence capabilities which governments rarely possess. Locating bases where the terrorist organization maintains some facilities is not sufficient. For reasons of political reputation as well as of effective deterrence, the United States must be able to demonstrate conclusively that the victims of a military attack were responsible for the crimes of which they were accused. The Secretary of State's argument that innocent lives may be sacrificed if some of the guilty are punished is ill-conceived. Military decision makers are fully aware of this limitation, and their awareness has inhibited the resort to force. At the same time, this requirement—that the adversary be identified and located with reasonable precision—makes it tempting to blame states. Nonstate terrorist organizations rarely possess the territory or interests against which one can conveniently retaliate. States, on the other hand, are fixed targets and perhaps more sensitive to counterforce, since they have more to lose.

The policy of retaliation is often justified on the basis of the assumption that punishment acts as a deterrent to future terrorism. This assumption may not be realistic. A state deters an adversary by influencing his value calculus. The terrorist must be convinced that the cost of carrying out his threat will be high: that the punishment will be not only swift and sure but also unacceptable. It is difficult to perceive correctly the effects of one's actions and words on the decision makers of other states. We cannot see the world through the adversary's eyes. The likelihood of misperception is increased when dealing with terrorists, who are distinguished by the very fact that they do not share our values, frame of reference, or attitudes toward risk-taking. We do not understand the motivation of terrorists, and it is dangerous to assume a perfect strategic rationality to their actions. The governments which support terrorism may be more easily deterred, but this is uncertain, and not all terrorists depend on state sponsorship.

The potential outcomes of military action comport serious risks for American interests. The most immediate danger for the United States in the Middle East is escalation. Israeli policy against the Palestinians has led to wider conflict with Egypt, in the past, and with Syria, in the present. The Israeli invasion of Lebanon in 1982 was ostensibly a response to the attempted assassination of the Israeli Ambassador to Great Britain. The Jordanian civil war in 1970 was precipitated by Palestinian hijackings and threatened to draw in Syria and Israel, and along with them their respective superpower mentors. An even more ominous precedent lies in World War I, a conflagration sparked by the assassination of the Austro-Hungarian Archduke by a Serbian nationalist at Sarajevo. The Austrian Empire regarded this act as an intolerable provocation and determined to put Serbia, whom they suspected of sponsoring terrorism, in its place. Given similar preconditions—rigid alliances, priority of the offensive in warfare, suspicion and conflict of interest—the precipitants of global conflict could also lie in a similar affront, equally minor in hindsight.

There is also the risk of failure, a lesson of history painfully learned in Iran. Failed intervention means lost lives and equipment, but it also means serious political embarrassment. It is difficult to disguise a mismanaged or miscalculated response, which can do more damage to reputation than inaction might have done. Intervening to rescue hostages risks their lives as well as those of their captors. Retaliation may backfire, as the United States discovered in Lebanon when Syria defiantly downed two Navy jets.

When errors occur in the context of small wars—over the Falkland Islands, for example—they may be ignored or obscured, but in a terrorist crisis the glare of publicity isolates and magnifies the consequences of miscalculation and accident.

In reminding ourselves of the dangers inherent in the use of force, we should also remember that there are no easy answers to this extraordinarily complex policy problem. Decision makers should recognize that the phenomenon of terrorism, although it appears to be a generalized condition, is not undifferentiated. Campaigns of terrorism are historically bound to a particular time and place. The objectives and methods of a terrorist organization can only be understood in terms of their political context. Policies that might work against one terrorist group in one region will not necessarily work elsewhere. Although states do aid terrorist organizations they do not often direct or control their activities. Terrorist organizations are not mindless proxies of state interests but have individual identities.

American policy toward terrorism remains crisis-oriented. The terrorist incident generates a flurry of activity and concern that is dissipated as quickly as it appeared. Policy toward terrorism is temporarily front-page news. Within a week or so, however, public interest fades and terrorism returns to its usual spot low on the list of the nation's foreign policy priorities. Calls for retaliation are replaced by reminders of caution. In the Beirut hostage case, the fact that not all the victims of terrorism were freed is forgotten by the public. A series of reorganizations of the government institutions responsible for dealing with terrorism have not resulted in consistent high-level attention to the problem. This pattern of crisis followed by neglect—a pattern encouraged by the fickleness of media (especially television) attention—can induce complacency and a false sense of security. It contributes to the unpreparedness the United States showed in Lebanon. Just as the Marine commanders were convinced that their peacekeeping mission conferred noncombatant status (and did not perceive the possibility of being seen as an adversary in Lebanon), officials at the American Embassy in East Beirut assumed that relocating to the Christian sector assured its security. A state of permanent alert is not possible; the constant flow of indistinct and unreliable warnings in Lebanon inevitably encouraged what is known as the "cry-wolf" syndrome. However, false expectations about what is likely to occur make it difficult to distinguish between signals and noise. Surprise is what makes terrorism effective. Our beliefs about what to expect, as much as lapses in physical security, make us vulnerable to surprise. We should be routinely concerned with decreasing this vulnerability and wary of overreacting in the heat of a crisis.

The lesson of terrorism is that even the most powerful states cannot hope to control their environments. For the United States, almost all interests abroad now carry with them the risk of terrorism, especially where domestic authority is weak and the American presence both prominent and controversial. Isolationism, however, is no longer a feasible foreign policy alternative. The United States has no choice but international involvement. Terrorism is the reflection of a world that is disorderly, volatile, and unpredictable, and in which insecurity has become normal.

More importantly, terrorism is a calculated strategy of the weak and should be recognized and presented as such by American public officials and the news media. The tendency to describe terrorism as a new form of warfare, a "war in the shadows," glorifies a method of violence employed only by movements lacking more impressive resources. When the contemporary wave of terrorism began in 1968 with attacks on diplomats and hijackings of civilian aircraft, no one suspected that it would lead to a debate at the highest levels of an American administration over the wisdom of foreign military intervention. Should the United States use preemptive or retaliatory force against terrorist organizations or against their state supporters, the issue of international terrorism will have reached an unprecedented level of international significance. This is the final risk: that in responding to terrorism we transform it into the grand spectacle the terrorists sought all along and raise its practitioners to the status of mythic heroes or villains. Provoking the intervention of the U.S. military could be the most impressive achievement modern terrorism has claimed.

David Williamson, Jr.
Senior Fellow in Science and Technology,
Center for Strategic & International Studies,
Georgetown University

It has become a commonplace to decry U.S. inaction—or inability to act—in response to a variety of offenses loosely described
as "terrorism." It is also becoming a commonplace to forecast
sharp increases in such offenses, with emphasis on their epidemic
spread to the United States proper. Quite a range of prophylactic
measures are being proposed, debated, or implemented: the fortifi-
cation of public buildings, the bombardment of suspect installations, the increase in armed guards on aircraft and at facilities; the
development of policies focused on surgical strikes, preemption,
and neutralization; the use of military force and forces for civil police functions; the abridgement of legal and traditional rights and
entitlements; the redirection of national intelligence resources and
institutions. The record of recent violence aimed at U.S. interests,
directly or indirectly, is quite sufficient to justify the growing concerns, the mounting prophecies, and the expanding debate. However, it seems that the American gusto for labels and easy
generalizations may be a contributor to the very real problems of
coping with what is apparently a worldwide resort to violence as
an early rather than later means of social and political action. We
employ the general term "terrorism" to cover quite a range of activities that stem from differing motivations and aim at different
objectives. Just as there is no single behavior definable as
"terrorist," so there can be no single family of prescriptions to cure
the ailment.

One of the things that makes careless use of the term
"terrorism" dangerous is that it tends to confuse crime and technique, crime and motive, crime and criminal. There may be value
to a disciplined avoidance of the term "terrorism" when the events
involved are better defined by older terms: extortion, assault, murder, blackmail, maiming, assassination, arson, vandalism. These
are concepts of criminal behavior well understood everywhere,
and relate the perpetrator to the event within a reasonably coher-
ent construct of what is and is not acceptable. Similarly, when de-

scribing (or imputing) motives for criminal behavior, it might serve well to annunciate those at play, such as revenge, anger, hatred, publicity, overthrow of an established order, control of the actions of others, or religious or political conviction. When we are not specific but rely upon shorthand labels, we run the risk of not understanding either the event or its sources; in the absence of such understanding, wildly inappropriate or disproportionate responses are more likely to gain ground, crimes are more likely to benefit from a "Robin Hood effect," prophecies of disaster are more likely to become self-fulfilling, and fear of the unknown more likely to paralyze the political processes of the nation.

It is probably a truism that a difficult problem appears much more amenable to solution if broken down into its component parts. If terrorism is indeed an emotionally charged description of many problems, then perhaps attention to the individual pieces can help the identification of individual solutions or palliatives. This suggests that each case—whether past, current, or foreseen—should be analyzed in its own terms, should be treated as what it is rather than by formula. This approach avoids the political dangers inherent in rhetoric without action: an administration that fulminates and threatens but cannot act loses credibility with its constituents and incites attack from outside as being a safe target for criminal exploitation. Further, this approach is consonant with the idealistic American concept of law, which deals with crime on an individual rather than class basis and seeks penalties proportionate to the wrong done. This step-by-step approach makes less attractive such suggested options as the shelling of villages and camps, or the vengeful pursuit or out-of-hand execution of conspirators. It allows for measured responses at the international political level—if that is where particular criminal blame lies—with an eye toward both resolving underlying root causes and coercing states and institutions into accepting appropriate norms of behavior.

It seems clear that nations and organizations can be threatened, and made to conform to basic rules, at the risk of their being damaged or destroyed. For such cases—where states and organizations control the issues and the means—coercion is a normal and legitimate exercise of national power in the national interest.

It should, of course, also be recognized that threats and coercion have little if any effect on the actions of martyrs, madmen, heroes, and true believers. If we ignore the existence and persistence of such people, we are likely to be caught off guard again and again. In the analysis of violent political crimes today it does not seem sufficient to establish a single logical *cui bono* within a Western frame of reference; we have as yet little experience with cultures who measure martyrdom as a benefit and to whom local sectarian issues completely blank out larger national and global perspectives.

I have noticed recently two disturbing trends. There is a tendency, when describing the actions of groups, organizations, and states, to alter or shift, sometimes quite subtly, the standards of responsibility that otherwise underpin human relations in the West. We heard, just after the recent Frankfurt bombing, a radio description of the wounded: "Some military personnel and some innocent civilians." We are quietly building up walls of difference that should not exist between public perception of those on duty and those not; we are drifting toward a resigned acceptance that, in peacetime, it is more acceptable that military people be killed than civilians incommoded. Also worth noting is a tendency, when explaining terrorism in media coverage and the like, to run to the blackboard and point out in excruciating—and often accurate—detail just how in the future such-and-such a terrorist group, with these and those readily available tools, could take over New York, poison Los Angeles, decapitate the government, or paralyze the East Coast.

There is no master recipe for suppressing the variant and vagrant drives that find expression, *inter alia*, in acts we condemn as terroristic. There is room, however, for better understanding of the complex forces that operate at local scales throughout the world. For example, a careful weighing of the internal Lebanese power struggle and of its interaction with the political and religious influences of Syria and Iran might have provided a stark risk assessment: namely, that any formal U.S. presence could come under vicious, and likely successful, attack because the contemplated scope of action (the embassy, the Marines) would impede self-defense. Similarly, when Israel acts in ways inimical to the interests of local Palestinians or Lebanese groups, revenge or at least leveraged extortion against U.S. interests should be expected.

Timely, cool distancing of the U. S. from unacceptable policies of allies, partners, and non-enemies can reduce the danger of vengeful backlash or political coercion through criminal threats or acts. For example, not yet a source of international incidents, the black majority of South Africa seems to be undergoing the kind of societal stress that in other cases has been the genesis of violent underground movements. Influenced by nations with their own geopolitical axes to grind, and attracted naturally by U.S. policies that appear to ignore their perceived interest, South African black extremists might find U.S. targets politically palatable and technically easy.

Also, it is not too farfetched to look at the possibility of such self-generated infections of violence arising within the U.S. itself from minorities that have been unable to attain their perceived appropriate share of power in the society. The rhetoric of the Nation of Islam, the brooding sense of oppression of the American Indian Movement, and ethnic support of the I.R.A., should give us pause. Not only are we quite able to bring things upon ourselves unnecessarily, unfortunately we also seem unwilling to study the phenomenon and process of social dissolution in advance of its reaching critical conditions.

Based on past experience with attempts to organize "wars" on social problems—crime, poverty, pollution, diseases—centralized political action is not likely to succeed if waged against the symptoms of problems. Further, the higher the level of attention, the greater the likelihood of some apotheosis of common crimes and criminals. Every effort must be made to avoid, consciously or subconsciously, legitimizing the criminal acts of individuals because of purported noble causes.

In short, the U.S. and the world could probably benefit from a number of steps that relieve paralysis, quell hysteria, allow remedial action, and present obstacles to personal and national forms of illegitimate violence. The first of these must be the development of objective insight into the sources of friction, present and future, that lead to violence. This requires a combination of scholarship and intelligence examining evolving patterns around the world—and at home—within a disciplinary framework that identifies opportunities for relief ahead of crisis points as well as pinpointing the likely hotspots of the future. A second step follows from the first: include overt consideration of all these islands of discontent in the formulation of foreign and domestic policy, with some assessment of the "worst case" implications of continued instability. A third suggestion is that in policy councils and news coverage we treat events now lumped as "terrorist" as individual acts of social and political wrongdoing by states and/or individuals. Focus of public understanding and therefore public reaction on the particular actors in the case allows for full flexibility in all other cases. Each event should generate its own self-contained legal, political, economic, military, or police response.

As the United States begins to accept the endemic nature of violence fueled from very different sources, it can turn its attention to the issue of collective rather than individual security. For, in the end, it will be a common effort by advanced nations that will provide the best protection from violence masquerading as legitimate political behavior.

Terrell E. Arnold
Executive Director,
The Institute on Terrorism and Subnational Conflict,
and Consultant to the Department of State

The June 1985 hijacking of TWA Flight 847 by Shiite radicals once again focused national attention on the possible use of military force to deal with a terrorist attack. Nothing happened, and it is important to understand why. Initially the time seemed right: The hijacked aircraft was American; it carried numerous American passengers; movements of the aircraft were well-known; early indications in the beating and fatal shooting of U.S. Navy diver Stethem were that the hijackers were affiliated with the Iranian-supported Hizballah group that had bombed the U.S. Embassy and the Marine Barracks, therefore additional deaths could be expected; and the American public largely was primed for action.

Suddenly, however, the opportunity seemed to evaporate. The hijackers either had already planned it or they evolved an elaborate subterfuge that consisted of cycling the aircraft back and forth between two widely separated safe havens (Algiers and Beirut) and separating the hostages, keeping the crew on board the aircraft and farming out the passengers with Shiite friends in Beirut. In Algiers the hijackers could expect relative security from a regime with a record of sympathy for revolutionary causes and with an established intermediary role in efforts to free the seven other Americans held hostage in Lebanon. However, the hijackers evidently feared that even Algiers was not safe and left unexpectedly for Beirut when media reports reached them of U.S. military dispositions in the Mediterranean, suggesting that the U.S. might be preparing for an attack. In Beirut, the hijackers took advantage of widespread Shiite sympathy, particularly from the Amal group, which controlled Beirut International Airport, and of the immense difficulties of locating, much less freeing, hostages held in scattered locations throughout Shiite neighborhoods. In these circumstances, it became obvious that even a completely successful raid on the aircraft itself, to free the crew and recapture the plane, overcoming armed Shiite opposition at the airport in the process, would almost certainly mean the death or indefinitely protracted confinement of the other hostages.

During this 17-day ordeal, all the problems, the hard choices to be assessed in deciding whether to use force—the risks of casualties, offense to other countries and failure—were squarely put before the President and his advisors, and the issues were the almost daily grist of primetime television anchormen. But the debate really went nowhere. Prudent recognition of the limits on uses of military power in this case prevailed, and no attack or counterattack decisions emerged. Rather, once again, the greatest military power on earth was in a position where it was unable, or unwilling, to react forcefully or rapidly—frustrated by a small group of terrorists and their sponsors.

Unless there are radical changes in the nature of international terrorism and in the constraints that now exist on a forceful response, the future will be much like the past. Because I believe strongly that an essential, albeit limited role exists for the use of military force in combatting terrorism, I am far from delighted by this conclusion. I think, however, that in the wake of the TWA 847 case, and before we once again find ourselves in a hostage crisis, we must look squarely into the light, and the hardliners among us must shed their illusions about how much of this problem military force can handle.

Our first task in getting at the military role is to get rid of a common logical leap that ends in a completely unnecessary twist. Many people say nowadays that terrorism is low-level warfare, and therefore many hardliners say the response to it must be a military one. I agree completely that terrorism is low-level warfare. It is an insidious warfare because it is undeclared, it is usually pursued in secret until an attack is actually carried out, and even after the attack it is often difficult to identify the enemy. Warfare by terrorist tactics has become a calculated policy instrument of several states, and in fighting back we may already be engaged in the nearest thing to World War III our generation will ever see. It does not necessarily follow, however, that the best answer to this challenge, or the one we can most reliably deliver, is a military response. Nor does the fact that many terrorist attacks are against military personnel and facilities make the case any stronger. Appearing to insist on using military force and seeing it as *the* solution rather than uses of police power puts us frequently at odds with our friends and allies, unduly complicates our own national decision processes, and arouses unwarranted expectations in the public mind.

As we saw once again in the attempt to resolve the TWA 847 hijacking, international cooperation is essential to the management of any international terrorist incident, and some agreement on the essential character of terrorism and the remedies for it is an important step in getting that cooperation. Where we and our closest friends and allies most obviously disagree (or more precisely, where we have been making them most uncomfortable) is on the issue of the role of military force. Several friendly governments—Great Britain, Germany, France, Italy, Israel, and others—maintain military or paramilitary counterterrorism forces. Germany has used its forces abroad to rescue hostages on an aircraft at Mogadishu, Somalia. Great Britain, of course, uses military forces to combat I.R.A. terrorist activities in Northern Ireland, an internal part of the United Kingdom. Israel uses its defense forces to combat terrorism in the Middle East region and pulled off the famous rescue at Entebbe. There are other examples. By and large, however, at home most Western governments consider terrorism a civil police responsibility and use military resources only sparingly to combat it. It is most unlikely, therefore, that any of these governments would ever look favorably on another country—not their ally the United States or any other—sending in military forces to preempt their management of a civil police matter or to substitute for their own forces in managing a terrorist incident on their soil. (The same is also true, of course, of Third World and Eastern bloc countries.) Thus, the fact that the great majority of international terrorist attacks against our people and facilities occur abroad, and many of them in friendly countries, makes terrorism a peculiarly awkward target for a U.S. military response.

Inside the United States, force is always available to us as a means to resolve terrorist incidents or to head them off, but the most cumbersome form of that force is military. The reasons for that begin with the fact that terrorism is a crime: terrorist attacks—such acts as assassination, bombings, assault, kidnapping, hostage-taking, threats, and extortion—are crimes against persons that are covered in criminal statutes. On this point, we are in complete agreement with other Western governments. Appropriate responses to such attacks are routinely covered in guidance given to civil police authorities, including rules of engagement for the use of deadly force. From the beginnings of our constitutional system, however, Americans have been suspicious and wary about uses of the armed forces to enforce civil law. Thus, so-called *"Posse Comitatus"* restrictions that now exist in Federal law bar the use of military force to deal with a terrorist attack, unless the President makes a determination that the facts of a specific case warrant military intervention. Such determinations inevitably are politically sensitive and time-consuming, and the requirement to make them at the present time effectively rules out use of military force as a first line of reaction to terrorist attacks at home.

Federal, state and local capabilities and policies have been generally adequate to deal with terrorism as we are now experiencing it in the United States. Terrorist attacks in the United States have declined in recent years, running counter to the trends in the number and the violence of attacks against American people and facilities abroad. The F.B.I. attributes this fact to the preemptive value of good investigative police work and to the deterrent value of timely arrests. Recent disruption of a Libyan plot to undertake assassinations of other Libyans in the United States, and of a Sikh plot to assassinate Indian Prime Minister Gandhi during his visit to the United States, are good examples of effective investigative work.

The keys to the ability of domestic law enforcement agencies to deal with terrorism are skilled personnel, regular exercise and training, readiness, good intelligence, and clear rules of engagement. Groups such as the F.B.I.'s Hostage Rescue Team and the Special Weapons and Tactics (SWAT) teams of various urban police organizations are doing a creditable job of providing skilled people and the training programs needed to maintain readiness. Experience with providing security to the 1984 Summer Olympics in Los Angeles improved existing procedures to assure effective cooperation among Federal, state and local authorities, and the intelligence gathering and sharing practices developed for that purpose represent an important net addition to national capability.

Domestic counterterrorism forces are ready to act on very short notice, but a key feature of their readiness is a clear set of rules about using deadly force. Federal, state and local police authorities generally are permitted to use deadly force to save lives and to prevent harm to themselves or to others. These rules are not debated each time a crisis arises, they are well established, and they are understood by police officers everywhere.

Our military counterterrorism forces are equally skilled, trained, exercised, and equipped as anything we have on the domestic police level. The principal differences between civil and military preparedness to deal with a terrorist incident are in readiness and rules of engagement.

Judging from performance in several deployments I am aware of during the past three years, our military counterterrorism forces are very quick off the mark to get evaluation and planning teams on their way, usually within hours of the start of an incident. Deployment of an attack team, however, can take anything from three to five days.

The sources of this seemingly unconscionable delay lie with the physical readiness of the attack force, the bureaucratic readiness of the decision makers, and the political circumstances surrounding each incident. The primary damper on physical readiness appears to be the need to make a host of last minute decisions about team composition, weapons, dress, communications and related issues, and then to rehearse the team in coping with detailed aspects of the specific incident in progress. In effect, our counterterrorism attack teams are ready for a generic incident, but it may take as much as 72 hours to get a team ready for a specific situation. Attack teams with capabilities and equipment for dealing with the great majority of terrorist incidents are on standby at all times, but as things are now done the decision to deploy an attack team does not begin until after an incident starts.

Decisions to deploy forces can take many hours or days, particularly if the case, as is frequent, involves several governments and the incident is occurring in a politically sensitive location. The combination of decision and deployment time routinely will go over 24 hours for an incident inside the Western Hemisphere, and it will go longer for events halfway around the world. As a result of such delays in deployment, precious elements of operational security, surprise and tactical opportunity are lost while our forces rehearse and await instructions. Failure to be at the scene in a timely way is effectively to render our counterterrorism forces useless.

Many of these problems could be solved and a higher state of actual readiness achieved by making the initial deployment decision practically automatic and by packaging the counterterrorism force around a concept like the football special team. The team on the field at any one time consists of eleven members, but that team is configured differently for differing offensive and defensive tactical situations. In training sessions and practice games each important configuration of the team is worked out and rehearsed so that the players coordinate well with each other in each team makeup.

Applying this concept to a counterterrorism program, strike teams could be designed, trained and equipped to deal with a broad range of attack situations related to a given type of terrorist incident. The skills needed to deal with specific variations of such an incident would be included, special teams would be built up in modular style, and the various scenarios for such an incident would be rehearsed with the necessary special teams. Like their football counterpart, these strike teams would work together and train together. When an incident or a preemptive operation calls for a strike team, the overall team would deploy with the full array of skills needed to deal with the broad category of incident and related contingencies, but the special team actually used in an attack would depend on the situation at the time.

Overall strike force teams could be developed for each broad category of terrorist situation. These forces would be kept as lean as possible, but each team would be complete with all its leadership, special skills and equipment, foreign affairs agency representatives, and necessary transportation included in the package.

As an illustration, such an overall team for a hostage barricade situation could be made up of diplomatic and other liaison personnel, intelligence gatherers and analysts, negotiators, psychiatrists, shooters, explosive ordnance specialists, communications and other electronic technicians, and specialists in terrorist weapons and tactics. It would be supported by dedicated aircraft and ground personnel, and it would be kept ready to deploy to an advance site within four to six hours.

Enroute to an incident, the team would review various mockups of the problem they expect at the other end. Any details on development of the incident, activities at the site, physical layouts, area and route maps, and the like would be studied. Continuous contact with observers (possibly embassy or military base personnel) would keep the team up to date on developments, as well as on any new intelligence that might affect planning. Configurations of the team needed to deal with various contingent situations would be discussed and assessed as to utility at the scene but the final call on how the attack team would be configured would be kept in abeyance until the last feasible moment.

This team could be deployed almost immediately on receipt of the announcement of an incident; it would go equipped on a premise that it might be used, and it would be tailored as carefully as advance information would permit. Any final decision on actually employing combat elements of such a team, however, would be made, as now, independently of the decision to deploy. While the team is en route, other important concerns could be pursued: accurate and timely intelligence must be collected and assessed. The risks of casualties—to strike team members, hostages, or bystanders—must be evaluated. Political considerations must be reviewed and weighed in any final decision to employ force to resolve the incident. To assure that such factors get fully taken into account, the separateness of deployment and employment decisions could even be reinforced to avoid any suggestion that moving the team implied any approval to use it.

Finally, the rules of engagement for combat elements of this team must be as clearly preordained as the rules now are for civil police. When an incident is in progress, there is no time to debate and reformulate such rules. In putting the special team together, we need to be absolutely sure that no doubts exist, among our counterterrorism forces, the public, the Congress, or abroad as to what the rules of engagement are for responding to a terrorist attack. Once our counterterrorism forces are committed to deal with an incident or to preempt one, the rules of engagement must permit them to use whatever force is needed to assure that they will win. Combat rules of engagement, not peacetime rules, must apply.

The United States is already very close to having these capabilities and arrangements at hand. We must, however, make decisions on deployment, and sharply cut pre-deployment preparation time, to take full advantage either of existing capabilities or of the special team concept.

Several benefits would accrue from adopting these concepts and from posturing our counterterrorism forces accordingly. *First*, the actual state of readiness, including equipment of special forces presently dedicated to counterterrorism activities, could be enhanced through increased rehearsal directed toward an immediate deployment. *Second*, with the deployment decision already made the team could be moved toward an advance pre-position on a schedule closely keyed to the development of the terrorist incident and therefore able to exploit the tactical situation in the event an employment decision is made. *Third*, with key friendly governments advance arrangements could be worked out for pre-position, transit, or staging of the overall team, or elements of it and equipment, on an expectation that the broad size and the shape would be predictable. *Fourth*, general public awareness of U.S. intent to deploy and possibly to use such teams in the event of terrorist incidents against us, or on the request of other governments, would spread some unease among terrorist groups and their sponsoring governments. *Finally*, the occasional, very judicious use of combat elements of such a team where American lives are at stake would make the point that deployment is not a mere show of force and would give U.S. counterterrorism forces a deterrent value which, to date, they have not achieved.

This approach is not magic. It will not remove the basic political, intelligence, and risk constraints that faced U.S. leadership during the 847 crisis, nor will it remove the limitations on uses of military forces in any country where we are not at war. Nor would I expect such an approach to increase greatly the number of instances in which U.S. counterterrorism forces are deployed and actually used, because the public and the Congress are unlikely ever to be enamored of the idea of using U.S. forces abroad against terrorist targets. Moreover, other governments cannot be expected to become any more receptive than they now are to the idea of some other government using military force in their territory. Those are all matters which must be addressed on a case-by-case basis now and in the future, and they usually will pose severe limits on uses of force.

What we can get out of this kind of effort is a greatly heightened national state of readiness to respond to terrorist attacks. With that, perhaps we can defend ourselves against the losses of speed and responsiveness now caused by our habit of delaying and debating any decision to use military force. That in itself will help a great deal, because as things presently work, by the time we make a decision to deploy even the planning and assessment elements of our team, most terrorist incidents have already been going long enough to have become intractable, highly public, controversial, and difficult to manage. If we continue on that path, it is predictable that the terrorists will win the next rounds, as they clearly have won several in the recent past.

BIBLIOGRAPHY

An asterisk (*) preceding a reference indicates that the article or part of it has been reprinted in this book.

BOOKS AND PAMPHLETS

Terrorism in Europe. Alexander, Yonah and Myers, Kenneth A. St. Martin's Press. '82.

Hitler's children: the story of the Baader-Meinhof terrorist gang. Becker, Jillian. Lippincott. '77.

Terrorism and the American response. Buckelew, Alvin H. Mira Academic Press. '84.

The crimson web of terror (1st ed.). Chapman, Robert D. and Chapman, M. Lester. Paladin Press. '80.

Terrorism: the Soviet connection. Cline, Ray S. and Alexander, Yonah. Crane Russak. '84.

Guerrillas and terrorists (1st American ed.). Clutterbuck, Richard L. Ohio University Press. '80.

The media and political violence. Clutterbuck, Richard L. MacMillan. '81.

Executive security: a corporate guide to effective response to abduction and terrorism. Cole, Richard B. Wiley. '80.

Salvador. Didion, Joan. Simon and Schuster. '82.

Counterattack: the West's battle against the terrorists. Dobson, Christopher and Payne, Ronald. Facts on File. '82.

The terrorists: their weapons, leaders, and tactics (rev. ed.). Dobson, Christopher and Payne, Ronald. Facts on File. '82.

The U.S. government response to terrorism: in search of an effective strategy. Farrell, William Regis. Westview Press. '82.

Political murder: from tyrannicide to terrorism. Ford, Franklin L. Harvard University Press. '85.

Values in conflict: Blacks and the American ambivalence toward violence. Frye, Charles A. University Press of America. '80.

International cooperation to suppress terrorism. Gal-Or, Neomi. St. Martin's Press. '85.

Espionage, terrorism and subversion: an examination and a philosophy of defense for management (2nd ed). Hamilton, Peter. Peter A. Heims Ltd. '79.

Hostage. Hamilton-Paterson, James. Collins. '80.

Terrorism, political violence, and world order. Han, Henry Hyunwook. University Press of America. '84.

The new terrorism: politics of violence. Harris, Jonathan. Julian Messner. '83.

Terrorists and freedom fighters. Hayes, David. Wayland. '80.

The real terror network: terrorism in fact and propaganda (1st ed). Herman, Edward S. South End Press. '82.

The effectiveness of anti-terrorist policies. Hewitt, Christopher. University Press of America. '84.

Terrorism, international crime, and arms control. Hippchen, Leonard Joseph and Yim, Yong Soon. Thomas. '82.

Guerrilla and terrorist organisations: a world directory and bibliography. Janke, Peter and Sim, Richard. Macmillan. '83.

Terrorism and personal protection. Jenkins, Brian Michael. Butterworth Publishers. '85.

Days of wrath: the ordeal of Aldo Moro, the kidnapping, the execution, the aftermath. Katz, Robert. Doubleday. '80.

The longest war: Northern Ireland and the IRA. Kelley, Kevin. Brandon, Lawrence Hill. '82.

The war against terrorism. Livingstone, Neil C. Lexington Books. '82.

Fighting back: winning the war against terrorism. Livingstone, Neil C. and Arnold, Terrell E. Lexington Press. '85.

Terrorism: a challenge to the state. Lodge, Juliet. St. Martin's Press. '81.

Transnational terrorism: a chronology of events, 1968–1979. Mickolus, Edward F. Greenwood Press. '80.

Terrorism, the media, and the law. Miller, Abraham H. Transnational Publishers. '82.

Punishing international terrorists: the legal framework for policy initiatives. Murphy, John Francis. Rowman & Allanheld. '85.

Terror in Ireland: the heritage of hate. O'Ballance, Edgar. Presidio Press. '81.

Victims of terrorism. Ochberg, Frank M. and Soskis, David A. Westview Press. '82.

Hydra of carnage: the international linkages of terrorism: the witnesses speak. Ra'anan, Uri. Lexington Books. '85.

Terrorism: past, present, future. Raynor, Thomas P. F. Watts. '82.

Violence as communication: insurgent terrorism and the Western news media. Schmid, Alex Peter and Graaf, Janny de. Sage. '82.

Responding to the terrorist threat: security and crisis management. Shultz, Richard H. and Sloan, Stephen. Pergamon Press. '80.

The terror network: the secret war of international terrorism (1st ed.). Sterling, Claire. Holt, Rinehart, and Winston. '81.

The politics of terrorism (2nd ed, rev, and expanded). Stohl, Michael. M. Dekker. '83.

The state as terrorist: the dynamics of governmental violence and repression. Stohl, Michael and Lopez, George A. Greenwood Press. '84.

International terrorism: how nations respond to terrorists. Waugh, William L. Documentary Publications. '82.

British perspectives on terrorism. Wilkinson, Paul. Allen & Unwin. '81.

Terrorism: international dimensions, answering the challenge. Wilkinson, Paul. Institute for the Study of Conflict. '79.

Fear of fear: a survey of terrorist operations and controls in open societies. Wolf, John B. Plenum Press. '81.

International terrorism. Wolfgang, Marvin E. Sage Publications. '82.

PERIODICALS

Held hostage by terrorism. America. 153:22. Jl. 20–27, '85.

Fear and trembling: terrorism in three religious traditions. Rapoport, David C. The American Political Science Review. 78:658–77. S. '84.

*Prime-time terror. Morrison, Micah. American Spectator. 18:12+. S. '85.

*Statements about terrorism. Jenkins, Brian M. The Annals of the American Academy of Political and Social Science. 463:11–19. S. '82. Discussion. 463:19–23. S. '82.

Terrorism: safety tips. Dunn, Donald H. Business Week. 109–10. Jl. 8, '85.

How the sanctions against Libya could fall flat. Rossant, John. Business Week. 47. Ja. 20, '86.

Terrorism tempts TV to waive noble right. Wall, James M. The Christian Century. 102:635–6. Jl. 3–10, '85.

TV hostage coverage cooled hot heads (discussion of July 3-10, 1985 article, Terrorism temps TV to waive noble right). Wall, James E. The Christian Century. 102:773. Ag. 28-S. 4, '85.

Fighting back. Ledeen, Michael. Commentary. 80:28-31. Ag. '85.

*Terrorism: the challenge to the democracies (address, June 24, 1984). Shultz, George Pratt. Department of State Bulletin. 84:31-4. Ag. '84.

International terrorism: a long twilight struggle (address, August 15, 1984). Sayre, Robert M. Department of State Bulletin. 84:48-50. O. '84.

Terrorism and the modern world (address, October 25, 1984). Shultz, George Pratt. Department of State Bulletin. 84:12-17. D. '84.

Combating international terrorism (statement, March 5, 1985). Oakley, Robert B. Department of State Bulletin. 85:73-8. Je. '85.

The new network of terrorist states (address, July 8, 1985). Reagan, Ronald. Department of State Bulletin. 85:7-10. Ag. '85.

*Fighting terrorism through law (address, July 15, 1985). Sofaer, Abraham David. Department of State Bulletin. 85:38-42. O. '85.

*Terrorism: overview and developments (address, September 13, 1985). Oakley, Robert B. Department of State Bulletin. 85:61-5. N. '85.

Europe: recovery & nihilism. Paz, Octavio. Dissent. 32:183-91. Spr. '85.

Enter Euroterrorism. The Economist. 294:41-2. F. 2, '85.

The IRA won't go away. The Economist. 295:59-61. Je. 29, '85.

No end in sight. Tasker, Rodney. Far Eastern Economic Review. 125:25-7. S. 20, '84.

Business copes with terrorism. O'Reilly, Brian. Fortune. 113:47-8+. Ja. 6, '86.

The end of the affair (murder of M. H. Kerr in Beirut). Ajami, Fouad. Harper's. 268:53-9+. Je. '84.

*Terrorism and the media: a discussion. Harper's. 269:43-7+. O. '84.

A will to live (S. Kaiser, Israeli woman whose family was killed by PLO terrorists). Hellman, Peter. Life. 7:80-2+. Jl. '84.

Disarmers of terror: the world's busiest bomb squad (Jerusalem police squad). Friend, David and Rosenberg, Robert. Life. 7:66-70+. D. '84.

City of rage: Qum, the heart of Shi'ite Iran, inspires a wave of holy terror (festival of Ashura). Haupt, Donna E. Life. 8:94-8+. S. '85.

The suicide terrorists (with editorial comment by Kevin Doyle). Miller, Robert. Maclean's. 96:2, 20-4. D. 26, '83.

Thatcher's close call (IRA's Brighton bombing; with editorial comment by Kevin Doyle). Laver, Ross. Maclean's. 97:2, 32-5. O. 22, '84.

The resurgence of terrorism. Lewis, Peter. Maclean's. 98:26-7. F. 18, '85.

The new Islamic whirlwind (special section). Maclean's. 98:22-5+. Ap. 1, '85.

A new reign of terror (bombing on Air India plane off Irish coast and at Tokyo's Narita Airport; special section). Maclean's. 98:20-6+. Jl. 8, '85.

Terror at ground zero—in two states (Israeli PLO raid). Posner, Michael. Maclean's. 98:47-9. O. 14, '85.

Journalists under the gun in Beirut. Friedman, Robert I. The Nation. 239:641-2+. D. 15, '84.

Reagan's 'good war.' The Nation. 239:667-8. D. 22, '84.

Desperately seeking solutions. The Nation. 241:1. Jl. 6-13, '85.

Rounding up the usual suspects. The Nation. 241:33. Jl. 20-27, '85.

Minority report. Hitchens, Christopher. The Nation. 241:72. Ag. 3-10, '85.

Teaching cops about terrorism (workshops run by J. R. Davis). Shapiro, Bruce. The Nation. 241:344+. O. 12, '85.

Confrontations of the third kind (Soviet involvement in international terrorism). Copeland, Miles. National Review. 36:28-9+. Jl. 27, '84.

K.G.B. connections (links to international terrorists, drug trade and organized crime). Ledeen, Michael. The New Republic. 188:9-10. F. 28, '83.

The new terrorism (state-sponsored terrorism). Krauthammer, Charles. The New Republic. 191:11-13. Ag. 13-20, '84.

Terror firma (views of G. P. Shultz on U.S. response). The New Republic. 191:5-7. N. 19, '84.

Undeclared war (Iranian terrorism). Pipes, Daniel. The New Republic. 192:12-14. Ja. 7-14, '85.

Terrorists and spies: Laqueur, Walter. The New Republic. 193:20-3. Jl. 29, '85.

Son of Brink's? (C. Chimerenga and the New York 8 to stand trial on alleged terrorist activities). Larsen, Jonathan Z. New York. 18:50-7+. My. 6, '85.

U.S. study is ready on terror policy. Boyd, Gerald M. The New York Times. p A7. Mr. 6, '86.

*The power of the fanatics. Friedman, Thomas L. The New York Times Magazine. 32-5+. O. 7, '84.

Notes and comment. The New Yorker. 61:17-20. Jl. 8, '85.

A freemasonry of terrorism. Newhouse, John. The New Yorker. 61:46-9+. Jl. 8, '85.

More madness in bloody Beirut (U.S. embassy annex bombing). Whitaker, Mark. Newsweek. 104:18–21. O. 1, '84.

Embassies under siege (U.S. diplomats). Anderson, Harry. Newsweek. 104:46–8. D. 10, '84.

*Ten ways to fight terrorism. Whitaker, Mark. Newsweek. 106:26–9. Jl. 1, '85.

The Lebanon Seven (Americans). Anderson, Harry. Newsweek. 106:28+. Jl. 8, '85.

Holiday of terror (attacks in Rome and Vienna airports). Anderson, Harry. Newsweek. 107:26–8+. Ja. 6, '86.

Banality and terror (terrorism as part of everyday life: Rand Corp. report). Gelman, David. Newsweek. 107:60+. Ja. 6, '86.

*Flake or fox? (M. Qaddafi). Watson, Russell. Newsweek. 107:14:20. Ja. 20, '86.

New modes of conflict. Jenkins, Brian Michael. Orbis (Philadelphia, Pa.). 28:5–16. Spr. '84.

Right-wing terrorism in Europe. Hoffman, Bruce. Orbis (Philadelphia, Pa.). 28:16–27. Spr. '84.

Terror, terrorism, and insurgency in Latin America. Radu, Michael S. Orbis (Philadelphia, Pa.). 28:27–41. Spr. '84.

Intelligence and counterterrorism. Ofri, Arie. Orbis (Philadelphia, Pa.). 28:41–52. Spr. '84.

A holy war in Pensacola (bombing of abortion clinics). Carlson, Peter. People Weekly. 23:20–5. Ja. 21, '85.

State-supported terrorism. Friedman, Robert I. The Progressive. 48:17–18. My. '84.

Terror network, U.S.A. (groups uncovered after Nyack, N.Y. Brink's robbery). Methvin, Eugene H. Reader's Digest. 125:109–19. D. '84.

Destination Teheran: anatomy of a hijacking (Kuwaiti airliner). Adams, Nathan M. Reader's Digest. 127:71–80. O. '85.

U.S.-sponsored terrorism (CIA manual distributed to Nicaraguan contras). Greider, William. Rolling Stone. 13–14+. D. 6, '84.

*Terrorism—what should we do? (symposium). This World. p 31+. Fall '85.

The horror, the horror (bombing of the U.S. embassy in Beirut). Kelley, James. Time. 121:28–31. My. 2, '83.

Again, the nightmare (bombing of American embassy in Beirut). Smith, William E. Time. 124:30–2+. O. 1, '84.

Horror aboard Flight 221 (Kuwaiti airline hijacked in Iran). Kohan, John. Time. 124:54–6. D. 17, '84.

The problems with retaliation (views of former CIA directors). Talbott, Strobe. Time. 126:20–1. Jl. 8, '85.

An eye for an eye (airport massacres in Vienna and Rome). Smith, William E. Time. 127:26–8+. Ja. 13, '86.

America: next target for terrorists? Chaze, William L. U.S. News & World Report. 96:24–6+. Ja. 9, '84.

Rash of terrorism ahead? Is U.S. ready? Kelley, Orr and Dudney, Robert S. U.S. News & World Report. 97:28–30. Jl. 16, '84.

We have no effective response to terrorism. Haig, Alexander Meigs. U.S. News & World Report. 98:46–7. F. 18, '85.

The FBI vs. domestic terrorism. Webster, William H. USA Today (Periodical). 112:10–13. Mr. '84.

Dealing with terrorism. Berry, Nicholas O. USA Today (Periodical). 113:40–2. Jl. '84.

*International terrorism (address, April 17, 1985). Casey, William J. Vital Speeches of the Day. 51:713–17. S. 15, '85.

A brotherhood of terrorism. World Press Review. 32:46–7. Mr. '85.

*Terrorism (special section). World Press Review. 32:35–40. S. '85.

State-sponsored international terrorism: the problems of response. Wilkinson, Paul. The World Today. 40:292–8. Jl. '84.